Mississippi's
Forests, 2006

Sonja N. Oswalt, Tony G. Johnson,
John W. Coulston, and Christopher M. Oswalt

United States
Department of
Agriculture

Forest Service

Southern
Research Station

Resource Bulletin
SRS-147

Author Contributions

Sonja N. Oswalt contributed the outline of the report; initial analyses and all text, tables, and figures not attributed to coauthors or acknowledged otherwise. Sonja was also responsible for compiling coauthor contributions and the majority of the photographs, and for completing two revisions of the report following peer review.

Tony G. Johnson contributed text, tables, and figures for the "Timber Product Output" section and the "Nontimber Forest Products" section.

John W. Coulston contributed the figures and map in the "Fragmentation of Forest Area" section.

Christopher M. Oswalt contributed the text for the "Ownership, Use, and Recreation—Results from the National Woodland Owner Survey" section and for portions of the "Glossary."

Sonja N. Oswalt is a Forester with the U.S. Department of Agriculture Forest Service, Southern Research Station, Forest Inventory and Analysis Research Work Unit, Knoxville, TN 37919.

Tony G. Johnson is a Supervisory Forester with the U.S. Department of Agriculture Forest Service, Southern Research Station, Forest Inventory and Analysis Research Work Unit, Knoxville, TN 37919.

John W. Coulston is a Supervisory Research Forester with the U.S. Department of Agriculture Forest Service, Southern Research Station, Forest Inventory and Analysis Research Work Unit, Knoxville, TN 37919.

Christopher M. Oswalt is a Forester with the U.S. Department of Agriculture Forest Service, Southern Research Station, Forest Inventory and Analysis Research Work Unit, Knoxville, TN 37919.

Front cover: top left, cherrybark oak plantation in Mississippi. (photo by Christopher M. Oswalt); top right, creek along the Natchez Trace Parkway, Mississippi. (photo by Sonja N. Oswalt); bottom, baldcypress swamp in Mississippi during high water. (photo by John Simpson, U.S. Forest Service). Back cover: top left, cherrybark oak stand in Mississippi. (photo by Christopher M. Oswalt); top right, cherrybark oak plantation in Mississippi. (photo by Christopher M. Oswalt); bottom, wild turkey toms in autumn forest. (photo by Steve Maslowski, U.S. Fish and Wildlife Service)

Pitcher plants in a Mississippi wetland. (photo by Donna Dewhurst, U.S. Fish and Wildlife Service)

Errors occurred during the preparation of Resource Bulletin SRS-147, "Mississippi's Forests, 2006," by Sonja N. Oswalt and others, as follows:

Page 8, right column, line 9 under "Extent of Area in National Forests" change loblolly-slash pine to longleaf-slash pine.

Page 19, left column, line 4 under "Timberland Area" change 12.5 million acres to 19.5 million acres. Also, on page 19 (right column) change text in Figure 23 from Total 12.5 million acres to Total 19.5 million acres. The proportions presented in Figures 22 and 23 remain the same.

Page 57, right column, on line 7 in tabulation, change "Annual mortality of all live" from 464.8 ± 19.1 with a Sampling error of 4.10 to 344.2 ± 12.1 with a Sampling error of 3.52; on line 10 in tabulation, change confidence interval for "Growing stock of net annual growth" from 28.7 to 29.1.

U.S. Forest Service
Southern Research Station --

Mississippi's
Forests, 2006

Sonja N. Oswalt, Tony G. Johnson,
John W. Coulston, and Christopher M. Oswalt

Cherrybark oak plantation in Mississippi.
(photo by Christopher M. Oswalt)

Charlie W. Morgan

Jimmy L. Reaves

The State of Mississippi celebrates a rich history rooted in its natural environment and a forest resource that is diverse and productive. The citizens of Mississippi receive multiple benefits from an extensive forest resource in the State, including timber and nontimber forest products; recreational opportunities, e.g., hunting, camping, and fishing; and clean water and air. With so much at stake and because the general public, policymakers, and resource managers need information that documents changes taking place in our forests, it is important to have the best available means for assessing the extent and condition of our forest resources.

Since the 1930s, the Forest Service, U.S. Department of Agriculture, has provided these means through the Forest Inventory and Analysis (FIA) Program, which conducts inventories of public and private lands, nationwide, at regular time intervals. Over the past 10 years, FIA has approached this inventory work in an exciting new manner by forming partnerships with State forestry organizations. The working partnership between the Mississippi Forestry Commission; the Mississippi Institute for Forest Inventory; and the Forest Service, Southern Research Station, FIA Program has improved and strengthened Mississippi's forest inventory. The quality of this report is a direct result of that sustained cooperation.

Because Mississippi's forests were impacted by Hurricane Katrina, the Mississippi Forestry Commission, the Mississippi Institute for Forest Inventory, and the Forest Service committed to an accelerated plan of completing the survey in 2 years instead of 5. Despite difficult field conditions, the employees of both organizations maintained their commitment to high-quality, efficient data collection throughout the inventory process. Additional assistance was contracted with trained field crew staff from other State forestry organizations and the Forest Service, FIA Programs. This assistance is highly appreciated and contributed to the completion in 2 years.

Because forests are much more than just tree volume and numbers of trees, this report includes information on forest health, ecological values, socioeconomic benefits, and biological diversity and includes an evaluation of a survey concerning the goals and objectives of Mississippi forest landowners.

It is with great pride that we present this information about the forests of Mississippi. It is our goal that the partnership between our organizations and the cooperative nature of this effort will continue to deliver the best information on the forests of Mississippi now and in the future.

Charlie W. Morgan
Mississippi State Forester
Mississippi Forestry Commission

Jimmy L. Reaves
Director, Southern Research Station,
U.S. Forest Service

Foreword

Forest Inventory and Analysis (FIA) is a nationwide program of the Forest Service, U.S. Department of Agriculture, and is authorized by the Forest and Rangeland Renewable Resources Research Act of 1978. Work units at Forest Service research stations conduct forest resource inventories throughout the 50 States. The FIA Program of the Southern Research Station in Knoxville, TN, is responsible for forest land inventories in the States of Alabama, Arkansas, Florida, Georgia, Kentucky, Louisiana, Mississippi, North Carolina, Oklahoma, South Carolina, Tennessee, Texas, Virginia, the Commonwealth of Puerto Rico, and other U.S. territories in the Caribbean Basin.

Immediately prior to beginning data collection in 2005, Mississippi was assaulted by Hurricane Katrina, which made landfall on August 29, 2005. The findings of this report reflect immediately noticeable damages caused by the storm, and present data against which future recovery can be measured. Additionally, this report represents the first complete forest inventory of Mississippi since 1994, a span of 11 years, thereby setting the stage for a new era of cooperative forest inventory in the State.

Additional information about any aspect of this survey may be obtained from:

Forest Inventory and Analysis
Research Work Unit
U.S. Department of Agriculture
Forest Service
Southern Research Station
4700 Old Kingston Pike
Knoxville, TN 37919
Telephone: 865-862-2000
William G. Burkman
Program Manager

Acknowledgments

The Southern Research Station and the authors gratefully acknowledge the Mississippi Forestry Commission for its role in collecting the field data. We also appreciate the hard work performed by Forest Service field personnel, and the cooperation of other public agencies and private landowners in providing access to measurement plots. Thanks also to the late Victor Rudis for contributions to the "Glossary" and "Inventory Methods" sections of the report. The authors thank Helen Beresford, Jeff Turner, and Jason Meade for their assistance in generating many of the estimates supplied in this report. Brett Butler, Earl Leatherberry, and Mark Brown also deserve thanks for supplying the results from the National Woodland Owner Survey for Mississippi. The authors thank the entire analysis section in Knoxville, TN, for contributions to the methods and statistical reliability sections of the manuscript.

Forest Inventory and Analysis cruiser measures the height of a tree in Mississippi. (photo by Andrew Edwards, U.S. Forest Service)

Contents

Contents

Flowering dogwood. (photo by Christopher M. Oswalt)

Page

American alligator. (photo by Gary Stulz, U.S. Fish and Wildlife Service)

Page

Text Tables

Multiple-use area on the Tombigbee National Forest, Mississippi. (photo by Sonja N. Oswalt)

Page

Appendix Tables

Alligator snapping turtle. (photo by Gary M. Stolz, U.S. Fish and Wildlife Service)

• The area of forest land in Mississippi is estimated to be about 19.6 million acres, or 65 percent of the total land base.

• The majority (72 percent) of forest land in Mississippi consists of naturally regenerated stands.

• Thirty-six percent of Mississippi's forest land is classified as loblolly-shortleaf pine forest, 27 percent is classified as upland oak-hickory forest, and 19 percent is composed of bottomland hardwoods.

• Weather-related events were the largest component of average annual disturbance (204,000 acres yearly) between 1994 and 2006.

• About 4 percent of live trees on Mississippi's forest land experienced some degree of damage due to Hurricane Katrina.

• Japanese honeysuckle (*Lonicera japonica*) is the most common nonnative invasive plant species in Mississippi, and occurs in every region of the State.

• Live-tree volume on timberland has increased 25 percent since 1994, from 24 to 30 billion cubic feet.

• Net annual softwood growth exceeded removals by 29 percent, and net annual hardwood growth exceeded removals by 22 percent.

• Aboveground biomass (dry weight) for Mississippi's forests averaged 42 tons per acre, or 816.6 million tons, statewide.

• The overwhelming majority (78 percent) of timberland in Mississippi is owned by private individuals not associated with forest industry.

• Mississippi landowners received > $10.8 billion for their standing timber between 1995 and 2006, or nearly $899 million annually.

• Total output of timber products, which includes domestic fuelwood and plant byproducts, averaged nearly 1.17 billion cubic feet per year between 1995 and 2006.

• During the latest survey period roundwood, harvested for saw-log and pulpwood production, amounted to 466 and 378 million cubic feet, respectively. These two products accounted for 86 percent of the total roundwood production for the State.

Creek along the Natchez Trace Parkway, Mississippi. (photo by Sonja N. Oswalt)

Flooded baldcypress-tupelo swamp in Greenwood, MS. (photo by Sonja N. Oswalt)

This report summarizes the findings of the eighth Mississippi forest inventory and represents a substantial cooperative effort between the Forest Service and multiple Mississippi State agencies. Measurements for the eighth inventory began in November 2005 and ended in September 2007. The inventory began at a very apropos time, following closely on the heels of one of the biggest tragedies to impact the gulf coast in the last century—Hurricane Katrina. Therefore, this report details changes to the forest resource since the seventh inventory, completed in 1994, and impacts caused by the hurricane-force winds, rain, and storm surge that accompanied the landfall of Hurricane Katrina.

Frequent users of FIA inventory reports will notice a change in the overall appearance of the report. This report has been structured in a manner that should appeal to a wide variety of audiences by grouping applicable information into headings closely aligned with the sustainability criterion and indicators described by the Montreal Process Working Group (Montreal Process Working Group 2005). The Montreal Process Working Group, formed in 1994, is a multicountry collaboration representing nearly 60 percent of the Earth's forests that is focused on the conservation and sustainable management of temperate and boreal forests. During a time when social, political, and scientific interests demand information on forest resources in a manner that can relate to a global audience, we strive to increase our relevance by presenting our data in a way that can aid in understanding the overall sustainability of the resource. Sustainability inherently includes the important socioeconomic role of Mississippi's timber resource in the State, and the desire to perpetuate that role into the future. Therefore, traditional timber product information appears in the "Socioeconomic Benefits of Mississippi's Forests" section of the report.

Cherrybark oak plantation in Mississippi.
(photo by Christopher M. Oswalt)

Hurricane Katrina made landfall in Plaquemines Parish, LA, on August 29, 2005. Katrina has been termed one of the most costly natural disasters in U.S. history, as well as one of the strongest hurricanes to make landfall on the U.S. coast in the last century (Graumann and others 2005). In addition to hurricane-strength winds, Katrina brought massive amounts of rainfall over a very short timeframe; a storm surge of up to 27.9 feet across southern Louisiana and Mississippi; extensive wind, rain, and related tornado damage throughout Mississippi, western Tennessee, and western Kentucky; and extended hurricane-associated precipitation as far north as the State of New York (Graumann and others 2005). Peak wind gusts associated with Katrina exceeded 50 miles per hour throughout the State of Mississippi (Graumann and others 2005).

Hurricane Katrina impacted a total estimated 7.8 million acres of forest land in Mississippi. That is equivalent to about 40 percent of Mississippi's total forest land acreage. Mississippi is divided into five survey units: South, Southwest, Delta, Central, and North (fig. 1). The area impacted was highest in the South Survey Unit, and was lowest in the North Survey Unit, as expected based on the path of the storm (fig. 2). While it sounds as though the hurricane devastated Mississippi's forests, statistics describing the area impacted are deceiving. Essentially, the "impacted area" describes any forest land where any visible wind-related damage occurred. Thus, even if damage was extremely minimal, e.g.,

a few broken branches here or there, the entire area was recorded as "damaged." Therefore, combining estimates of the total area damaged with estimates of individual tree damage helps to clarify the true impacts of the storm on the State's forest resources.

Less than 1 percent of surviving live trees experienced wind-related damage in all units except the Central and South Survey Units (fig. 3). In the Central Survey Unit, 1.5 percent of all live trees experienced damage, while 14 percent of live trees in the most heavily impacted South Survey Unit experienced damage. Statewide, 4 percent of all live trees on Mississippi's forest land experienced some degree of wind-related damage from Hurricane Katrina.

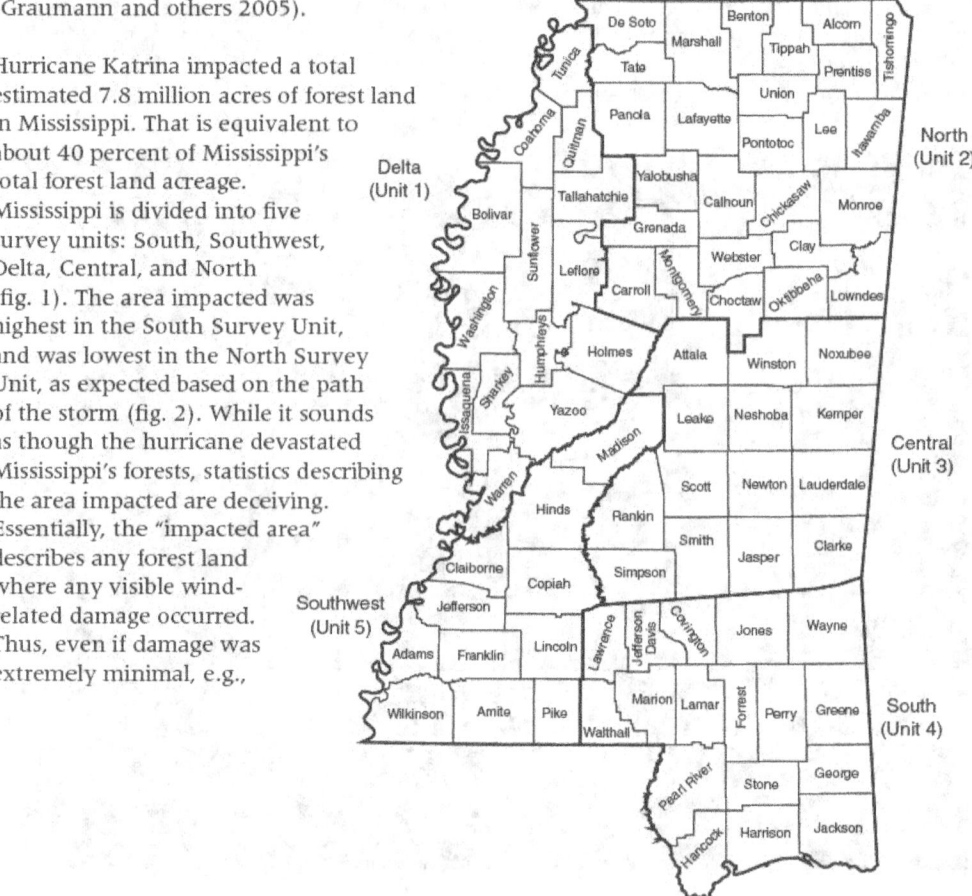

Figure 1—Survey units and counties in Mississippi.

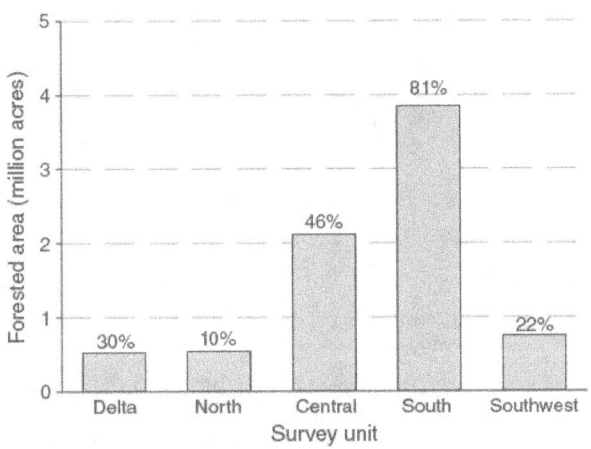

Figure 2—Forested acres impacted by Hurricane Katrina by survey unit with percent of all forest acres in the unit noted above the bars, Mississippi, 2006.

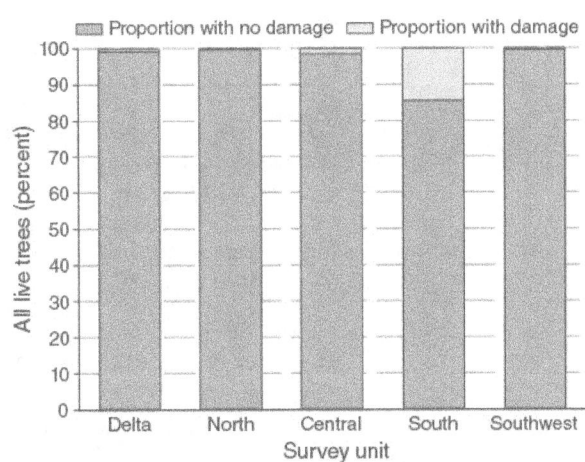

Figure 3—Proportion of all live trees ≥ 1.0 inch d.b.h. on forest land experiencing any wind-related Hurricane Katrina damage, Mississippi, 2006.

Trees killed by flooding in Greenwood, MS. (photo by Christopher M. Oswalt)

3

Forests play a vital role in Mississippi's economic, cultural, and biological landscape. The dependence of Mississippians on the forested landscape requires that attention be paid to the extent and condition of the forests. Although the term biological diversity (biodiversity) refers to all aspects of the forest ecosystem, from trees to insects to genetics, this report focuses solely on trees as they relate to forest biodiversity.

The area of forest land in Mississippi is estimated to be 19.6 million acres, or 65 percent of the total land base. Forest land has increased by 6 percent since the previous survey, conducted in 1994. Forest land is fairly evenly distributed across the State, with the exception of the heavily farmed Delta Survey Unit (fig. 4).

Trends since 1934 show that the Delta Survey Unit lost forest acreage between 1934 and 1987, a phenomenon that coincided with increased soybean, corn, and rice production in the Mississippi Delta and a well-known decline in bottomland hardwood forests (Kellison and Young 1997, King and Keeland 1999). Although the Delta still contains the least amount of forest land in Mississippi, total forest area has increased in that unit by 13 percent since 1994 and timberland has increased by 12 percent, a combined result of afforestation programs and cropland to forest land reversions as efforts to reestablish bottomland hardwoods increase (King and Keeland 1999; fig. 5). The Central, North, and Southwest Survey Units of Mississippi have gained forest land since 1934, and all FIA units in Mississippi have gained forest land acreage since the 1970s.

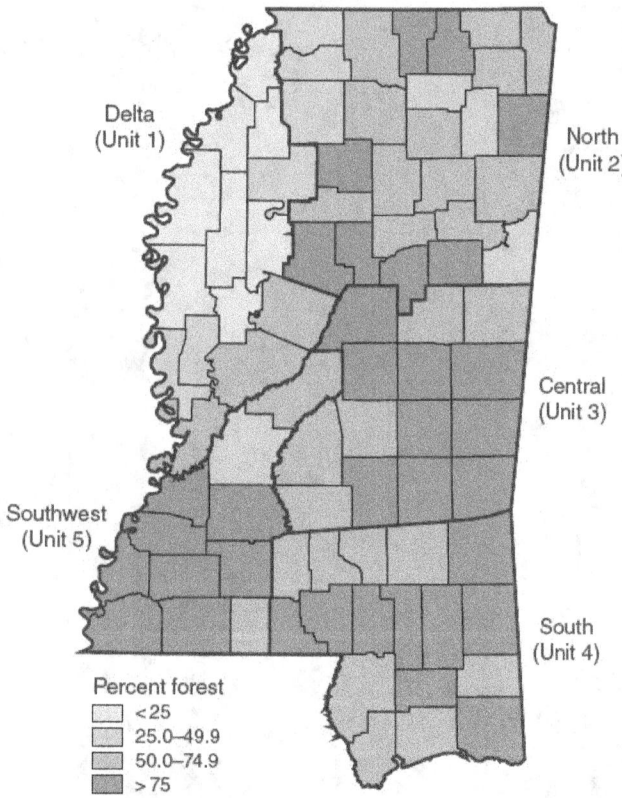

Figure 4—Percentage of land that is forested by county, Mississippi, 2006 (State average = 65 percent).

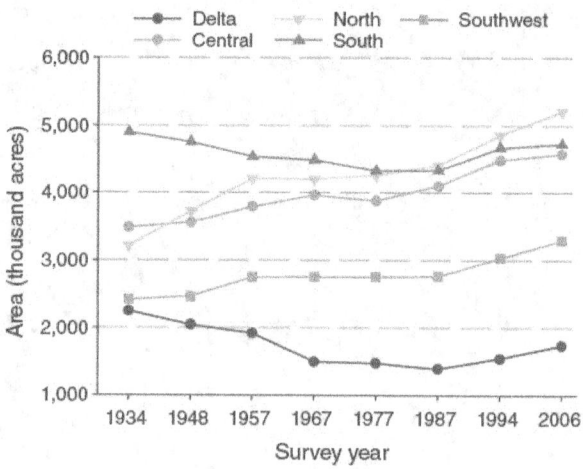

Figure 5—Changes in timberland acreage in Mississippi by survey year and survey unit.

Meeting of foresters to discuss southern hardwood forests in Vicksburg, MS. (photo by Christoper M. Oswalt)

Extent of Area by Forest Type Relative to Total Forest Area

Mississippi is well known for its lush pine forests. Thirty-six percent of Mississippi's forest land is classified as loblolly-shortleaf pine forest, while 27 percent of the forest land area falls into the oak-hickory forest-type group. The area of loblolly-shortleaf pine has increased by nearly 47 percent since 1994, while the area occupied by the oak-hickory forest type has declined by 8 percent. Nineteen percent of the forest land area is composed of bottomland hardwoods in the oak-gum-cypress and elm-ash-cottonwood forest-type groups, combined (fig. 6).

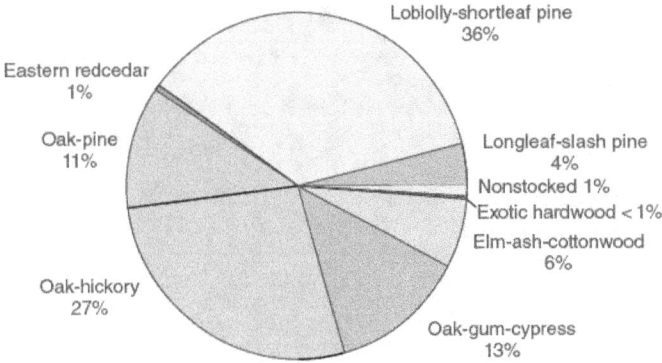

Figure 6—Percent forest land by forest type, Mississippi, 2006.

Mississippi's forests differ by physiographic unit and reflect topographic and climatic differences across the State. Forests in the fertile Mississippi Delta consist primarily of bottomland hardwoods, while central and southwest Mississippi support a fairly even mixture of oak-hickory and loblolly-shortleaf forests. In contrast, northern and southern Mississippi support predominately pine forest types, with some oak-hickory and bottomland hardwood forest types (fig. 7).

Extent of Area by Age Class, Stand Size, Forest Type, and Origin

Mississippi forests are comprised of a variety of age classes and successional states. The majority of forest land area occupied by southern pine forests (longleaf-slash, loblolly-shortleaf, and eastern redcedar) in Mississippi consists of young stands (1 to 20 years old), while a larger percentage of bottomland hardwood (oak-gum-cypress and elm-ash-cottonwood), and upland mixed pine/hardwood (oak-pine, oak-hickory, and maple-beech-birch) forest land area consists of stands older than 20 years (fig. 8). Very little forest land area in Mississippi is occupied by forests older than 80 years of age.

Sawtimber stands occupy nearly one-half (46 percent) of the forest land area in Mississippi—an increase since 1994 (fig. 9). Likewise, in southern pine forests, sawtimber stands occupy double the area of sapling-seedling stands (fig. 10). Upland mixed pine-hardwood stands appear to be experiencing some renewed regeneration, evidenced by a fairly large ratio of forest land area occupied by stands of small average diameters. Bottomland hardwood forest land area, while still predominately occupied by stands of large average diameter, appears to be experiencing an increase in regeneration. The area

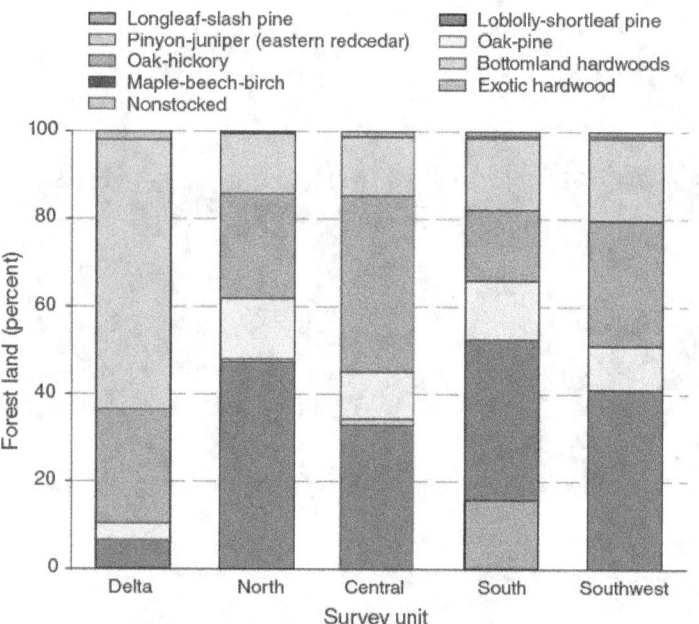

Figure 7—Proportion of forest land in each unit occupied by a given forest type, Mississippi, 2006.

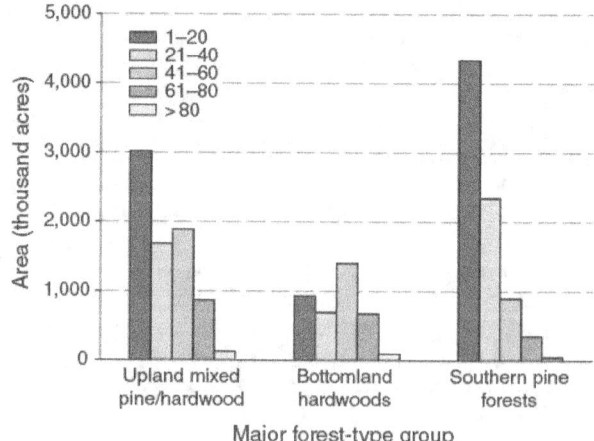

Figure 8—Extent of forest area by age class and major forest-type group, Mississippi, 2006.

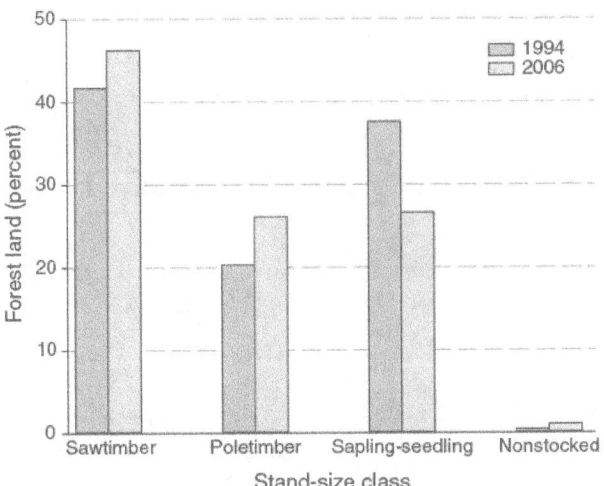

Figure 9—Distribution of forest land in Mississippi by stand-size class and survey year.

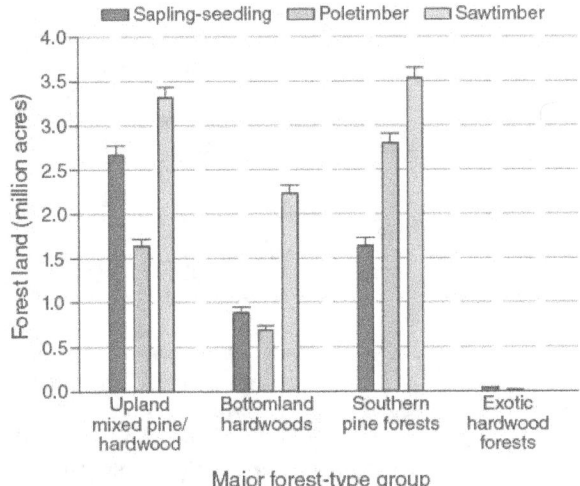

Figure 10—Distribution of forest land (±one standard error) in Mississippi by major forest-type group and stand-size class, 2006.

Cherrybark oak stand in Mississippi. (photo by Christopher M. Oswalt)

7

of bottomland hardwood forests in the sapling-seedling size class has increased by 93 percent since 1994, from 458,019 (±50,290) acres to 884,956 (±65,132) acres. This may be the result of reforestation and afforestation efforts occurring in the Delta region over the last decade (King and Keeland 1999).

The majority (72 percent) of forest land in Mississippi consists of naturally regenerated stands, and likewise, most major forest types consist primarily of naturally regenerated forest land. One notable exception involves southern pine forests, which are predominately (59 percent) regenerated through artificial means (fig. 11), reflecting the economic importance of pine plantations in the State. Overall, artificially regenerated acreage has increased slightly since 1994 (fig. 12).

Extent of Area in National Forests

Mississippi has six national forests totaling 1.3 million acres of forest land (fig. 13). About 10,000 acres are reserved, while the rest are available for multiple uses including timber production. Loblolly-shortleaf pine forests occupy the largest forest land acreage in Mississippi's national forests (471,576 acres), followed by oak-hickory forests (270,669 acres), and loblolly-slash pine forests (264,039 acres). Ninety percent of Mississippi's national forest forest land is of natural origin. Loblolly pine occupies the majority of the 10 percent of forest land that has been regenerated by human intervention.

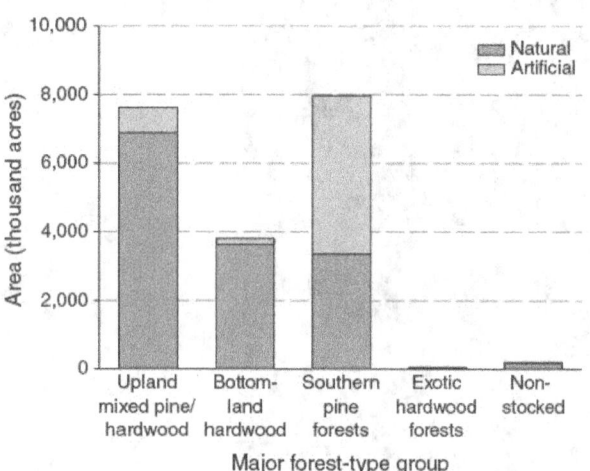

Figure 11—Area of forest land by major forest-type group and stand origin, Mississippi, 2006.

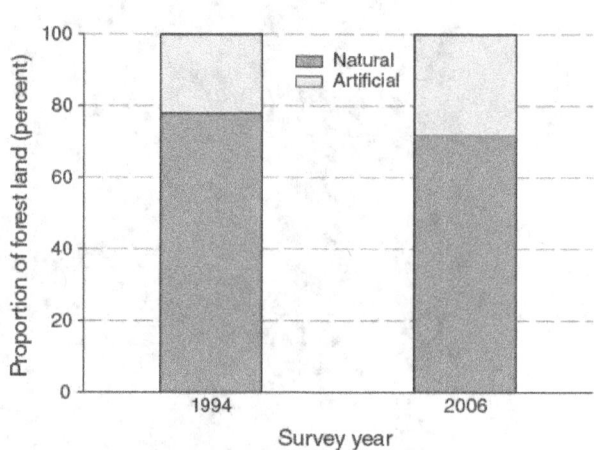

Figure 12—Proportion of forest land by stand origin and survey year, Mississippi.

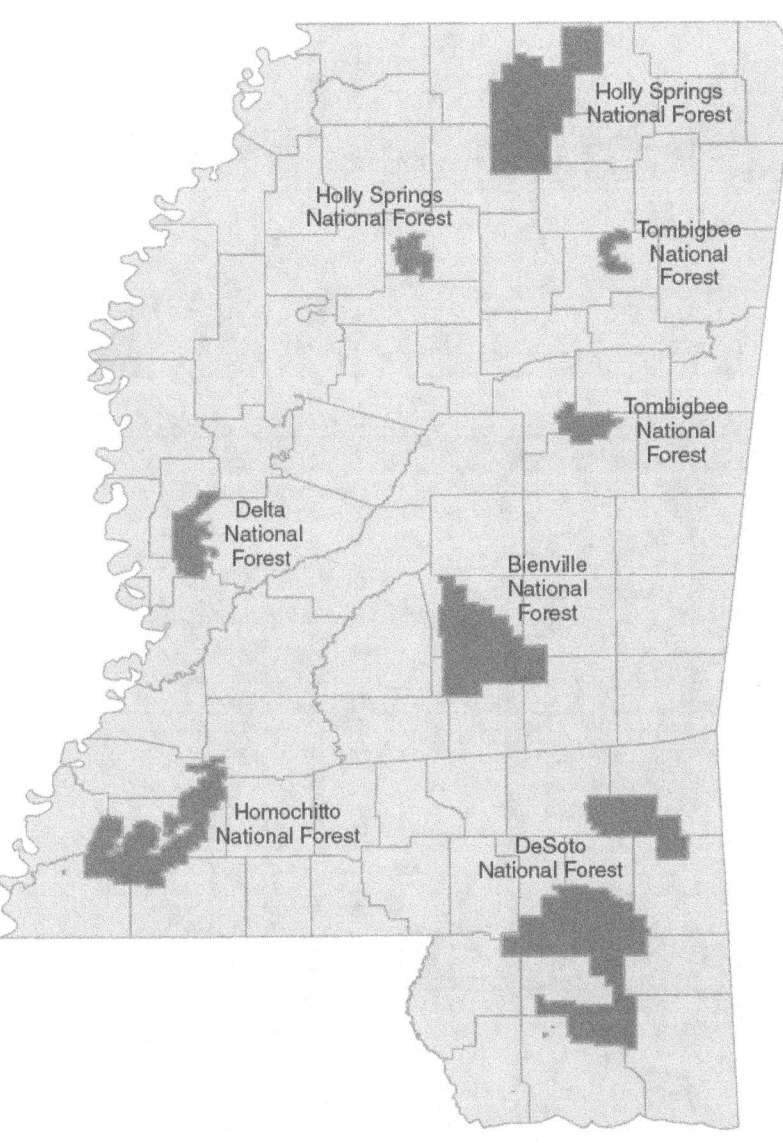

Figure 13—Location of Mississippi's national forests.

Tombigbee National Forest on the
Natchez Trace Parkway, Mississippi.
(photo by Sonja N. Oswalt)

Fragmentation of Forest Area

Fragmentation, or the division of forest land into increasingly smaller areas, can adversely impact ecosystem processes and/or biodiversity. Forests (interior, edge, or patches) occupy the majority of the land base in the South, Southwest, and Central Survey Units of Mississippi, while nonforest land uses predominate in the Delta and North FIA Survey Units (figs. 14 and 15; Riitters and

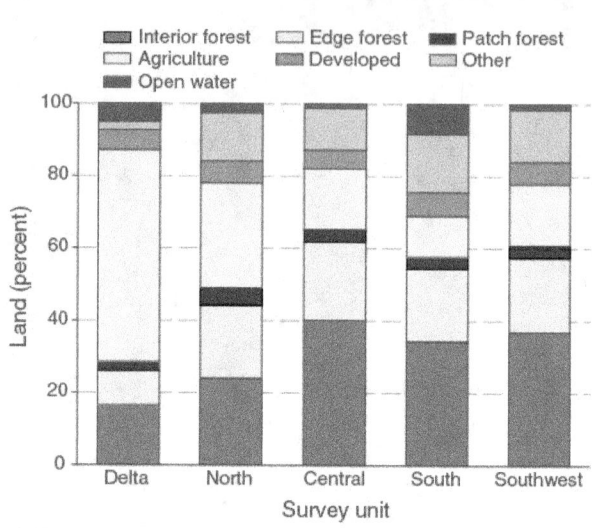

Figure 14—Land use by survey unit and land-use category, Mississippi, 2006 (Homer and others 2007, Riitters and others 2002).

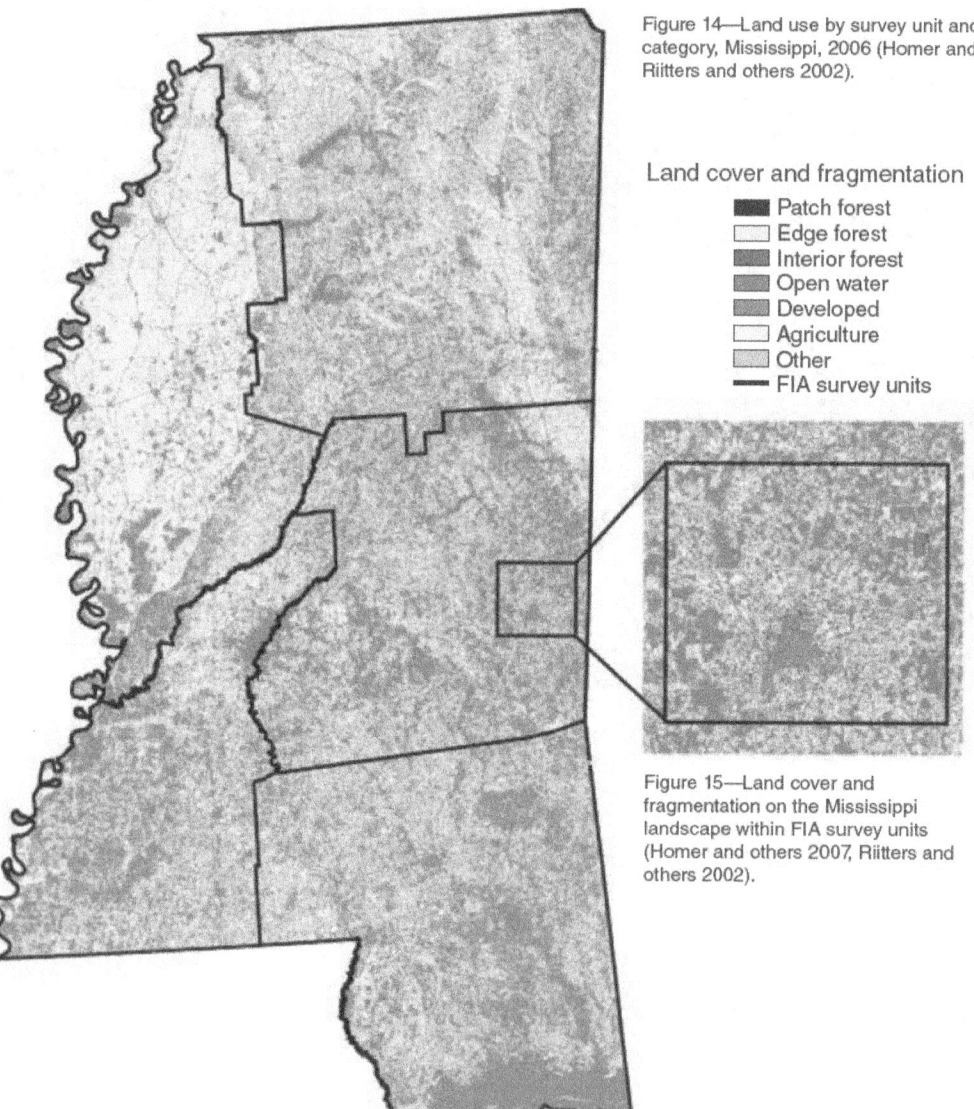

Land cover and fragmentation

- Patch forest
- Edge forest
- Interior forest
- Open water
- Developed
- Agriculture
- Other
- FIA survey units

Figure 15—Land cover and fragmentation on the Mississippi landscape within FIA survey units (Homer and others 2007, Riitters and others 2002).

others 2002). In addition to representing the smallest land area, forests in the North and Delta Survey Units are more heavily fragmented than forests in the other three FIA survey units, with slightly higher proportions of total forest land in edge and patch forests (fig. 16). The Central and Southwest Survey Units, in addition to having the most forest land area, have the least fragmented forests (fig. 16).

Agriculture is the primary nonforest land use across the State of Mississippi. Agriculture accounts for the majority of all land use in the Mississippi Delta and is the predominant nonforest land use in all but Mississippi's South FIA unit (fig. 17). Other land uses (bare land, scrub, shrubland, grassland, and herbaceous wetlands, as defined by Homer and others 2004) make up the primary nonforest land use in Mississippi's South unit. Urban development is also highest in the South and lowest in the Delta FIA units.

Disturbances as Instruments of Change

The development and structure of Mississippi's forest land is heavily influenced by the numerous natural and anthropogenic disturbances that occur across the landscape. Mississippi is subject to numerous weather events yearly, including hurricanes, tornadoes, floods, freezing rain and ice storms, and drought. For the period between 1994 and 2006, an estimated 323,000 acres were disturbed annually. The FIA Program defines ground-collected disturbance as an affected area at least 1 acre in size with mortality or damage to at least 25 percent of the trees. Weather-related events were the largest component of average annual disturbance (204,000 acres yearly) between 1994 and 2006 (fig. 18). Hurricane Katrina played a major role in disturbance events on the Mississippi landscape in 2005. However, Katrina was

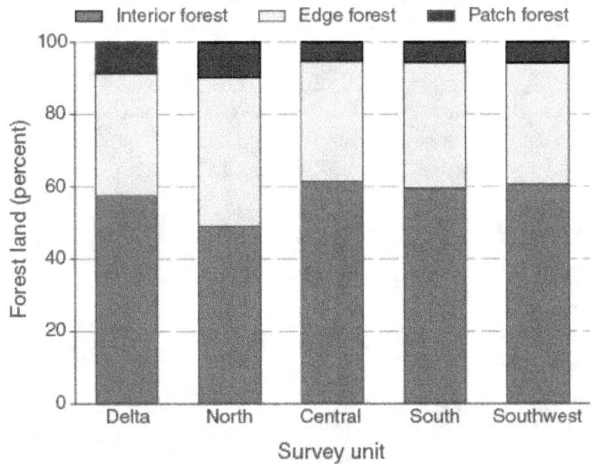

Figure 16—Proportion of forest land by forested landscape position and survey unit, Mississippi, 2006 (Homer and others 2007, Riitters and others 2002).

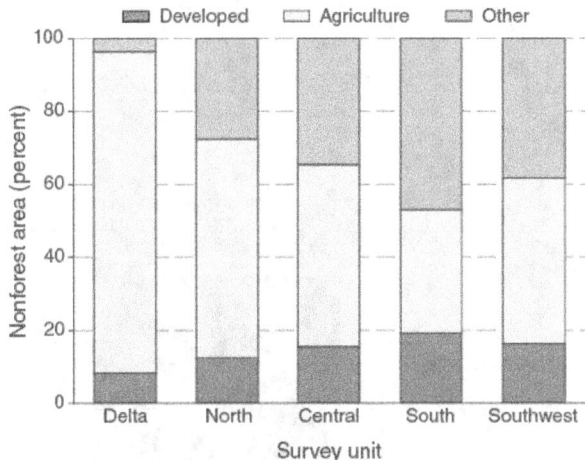

Figure 17—Proportion of nonforest area by land use type and survey unit, Mississippi, 2006 (Homer and others 2007, Riitters and others 2002).

only one among many storms that impacted the State between measurement periods. Six hundred and forty-six tornadoes, 38 hurricanes and tropical storms, 990 flood events, and 35 snow and ice events were reported in Mississippi from January 1, 1994, to March 31, 2006 (National Oceanic and Atmospheric Administration 2007). These disturbance events have had various degrees of influence on the trajectory of Mississippi's forests over the past 12 years. McNulty and Aber (2001) note that "the

impacts of these disturbances are highly variable," but are the "most important natural disturbance mechanisms for forest change in the United States." Although disturbances vary from extreme landscape-scale events like Hurricane Katrina to frequent small-scale events like canopy-gap formation, all disturbance events effect the composition of Mississippi's forests.

Tree Species Diversity

One hundred and thirty-seven tree species were measured in the 2006 inventory. Loblolly pine (*Pinus taeda*) and sweetgum (*Liquidambar styraciflua*) were the most frequently recorded species (live stems ≥ 1.0 inch diameter at breast height (d.b.h.); fig. 19). Estimates indicate a population of about 2.9 billion loblolly pine and 2.1 billion sweetgum trees across the State (table 1). Field crews recorded 86 species in the Delta unit, 96 species in the North unit, 106 species in the Central unit, 97 species in the South unit, and 95 species in the Southwest unit. Loblolly pine and sweetgum were the most frequently recorded species in each unit except the Delta and the South units. Sweetgum and sugarberry (*Celtis laevigata*) were the most frequently recorded species in the Delta unit, and loblolly pine and water oak

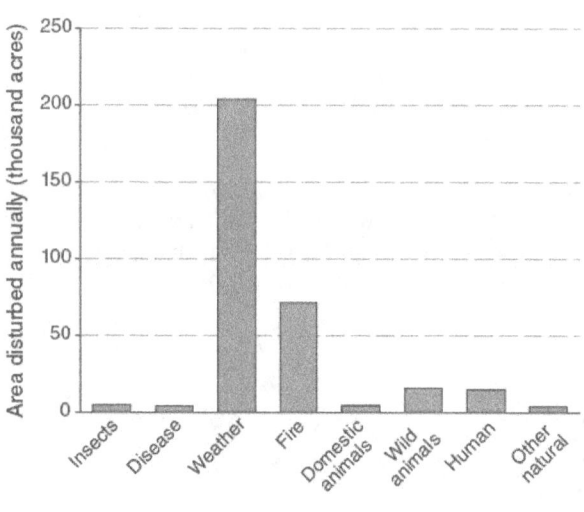

Figure 18—Area of forest land in Mississippi disturbed annually between 1994 and 2006 by disturbance category.

Baldcypress swamp in Mississippi during high water. (photo by John Simpson, U.S. Forest Service)

12

(*Quercus nigra*) were the most frequently recorded species in the South unit (table 1). Mississippi's forest land contains about 14.0 billion live trees ≥ 1.0 inch d.b.h.

While there are commonalities statewide with regard to species composition, e.g., the prevalence of loblolly pine across the State, most species have restricted ranges that relate to soils, climate, and other topographical characteristics. Many of these species are important to the economy of the State, or to wildlife resources. Some less frequent species may be more important ecologically than very frequent species. Indeed, the relative rarity of some species contributes to their importance in the State because the resources provided by those species are particularly limited. The distributions of four softwoods of particular ecological and/or economic importance are given in figure 20. The distributions of four hardwoods of particular ecological and/or economic importance are given in figure 21.

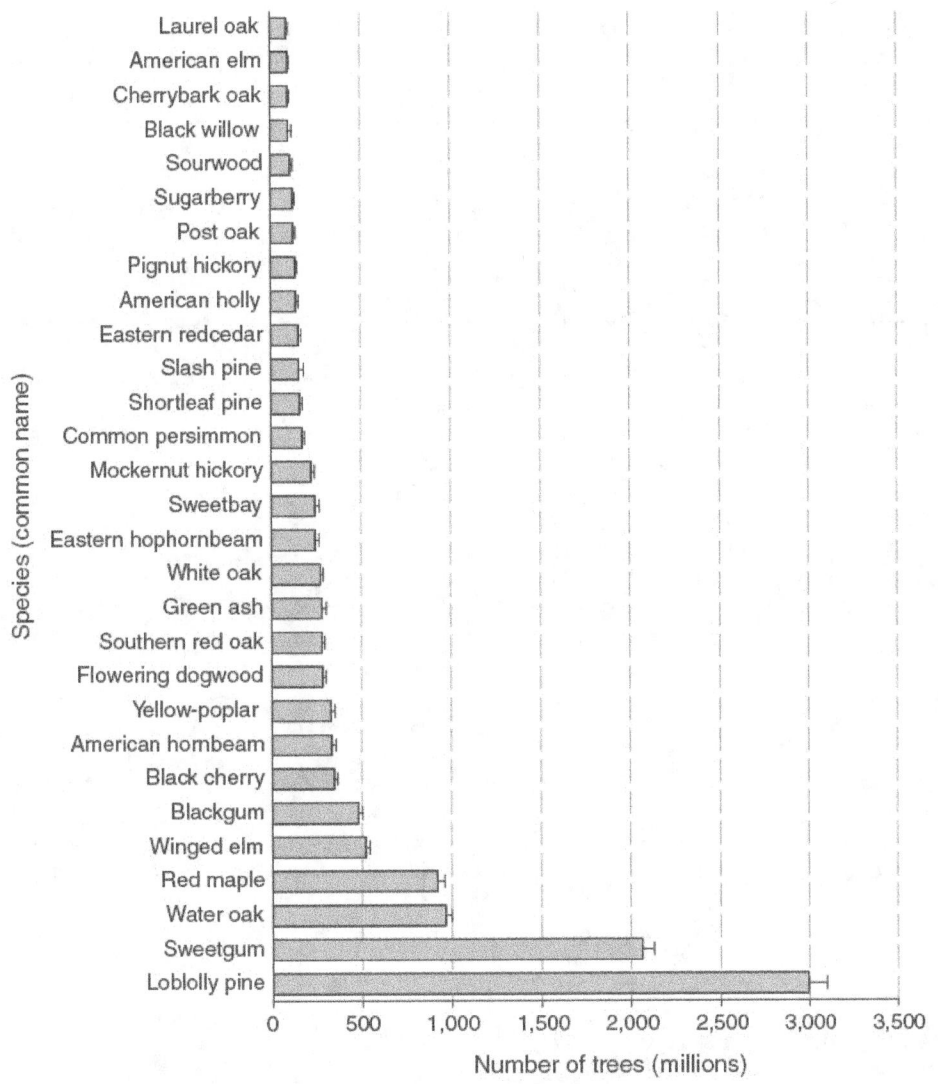

Figure 19—Estimated number of all live trees ≥ 1.0 inch d.b.h. (±one standard error) for common tree species in Mississippi, 2006.

Table 1—Tree species recorded on Mississippi forest land and number of estimated live trees > 1.0 inch d.b.h., by unit and statewide

Scientific name	Common name	FIA survey unit					Statewide total
		Delta	North	Central	South	Southwest	
				number			
Acer barbatum	Florida maple	3,973,821	4,988,208	519,619	—	1,627,618	11,109,265
A. negundo	Boxelder	25,566,561	19,814,012	10,352,173	2,339,728	15,788,700	73,861,174
A. pensylvanicum	Striped maple	—	—	446,198	—	—	446,198
A. rubrum	Red maple	26,969,461	288,095,367	268,870,492	280,083,394	54,937,928	918,956,642
A. saccharinum	Silver maple	424,633	2,167,665	1,999,713	—	75,242	4,667,252
A. saccharum	Sugar maple	106,927	877,090	—	—	—	984,016
Aesculus glabra	Ohio buckeye	446,403	—	446,198	—	—	892,601
A. sylvatica	Painted buckeye	—	—	446,198	—	—	446,198
Ailanthus altissima	Ailanthus	—	37,616	1,338,595	—	—	1,376,211
Albizia julibrissin	Mimosa, silktree	36,154	1,622,070	2,099,117	—	893,925	4,651,265
Amelanchier spp.	Serviceberry spp.	—	1,443,323	5,354,381	439,707	—	7,237,411
Asimina triloba	Pawpaw	4,074,667	1,405,708	8,557,950	483,545	5,523,921	20,045,791
Betula nigra	River birch	71,672	17,052,141	9,005,331	3,165,663	940,726	30,235,533
Carpinus caroliniana	American hornbeam, musclewood	27,249,857	68,408,754	107,723,890	38,786,606	88,608,331	330,777,439
Carya alba	Mockernut hickory	5,117,406	119,078,219	52,295,585	28,115,602	18,117,690	222,724,502
C. aquatica	Water hickory	22,421,142	2,096,202	4,962,709	2,093,163	1,278,826	32,852,041
C. carolinae-septentrionalis	Southern shagbark hickory	—	726,243	505,979	—	—	1,232,222
C. cordiformis	Bitternut hickory	1,337,093	3,035,111	2,719,858	—	3,446,007	10,538,069
C. glabra	Pignut hickory	6,808,777	59,525,210	41,115,263	3,876,336	23,830,852	135,156,438
C. illinoinensis	Pecan	7,901,788	6,090,608	221,289	591,459	6,529,304	21,334,447
C. laciniosa	Shellbark hickory	—	3,149,956	3,001,350	—	—	6,151,306
C. myristiciformis	Nutmeg hickory	—	—	517,838	—	—	517,838
C. ovalis	Red hickory	—	1,556,170	107,459	—	—	1,663,630
C. ovata	Shagbark hickory	1,924,850	18,573,686	7,226,022	38,818	37,621	27,800,996
C. pallida	Sand hickory	106,158	—	—	—	—	106,158
C. texana	Black hickory	70,772	3,368,113	999,856	74,117	71,234	4,584,092
Castanea mollissima	Chinese chestnut	—	—	37,600	—	—	37,600
C. pumila	Chinkapin	—	33,847	—	439,707	—	473,554
Catalpa bignonioides	Southern catalpa	106,158	—	112,801	38,818	—	257,777
Celtis laevigata	Sugarberry	62,342,538	13,915,724	15,824,714	2,280,550	26,459,126	120,822,652
C. occidentalis	Hackberry	1,589,612	37,616	1,648,120	36,001	656,738	3,968,087
Cercis canadensis	Eastern redbud	5,034,516	21,109,924	14,126,418	1,876,782	635,513	42,783,153
Chamaecyparis thyoides	Atlantic white cedar	—	—	—	3,360,336	—	3,360,336
Cladrastis kentukea	Yellowwood	—	—	—	—	981,386	981,386
Cornus florida	Flowering dogwood	13,809,190	92,799,451	87,972,605	60,530,315	28,314,572	283,426,133
Crataegus mollis	Downy hawthorn	440,795	—	892,397	—	—	1,333,192
C. spp.	Hawthorn spp.	3,608,350	468,569	8,526,397	9,898,124	—	22,501,441
Diospyros virginiana	Common persimmon	27,991,000	55,999,041	35,150,423	31,875,701	22,944,367	173,960,532
Fagus grandifolia	American beech	6,757,969	15,381,246	8,104,066	7,267,205	23,242,090	60,752,576
Fraxinus americana	White ash	1,813,724	16,235,615	6,847,385	2,404,166	5,877,589	33,178,479
F. pennsylvanica	Green ash	49,697,837	108,853,255	81,925,894	20,579,572	16,308,035	277,364,592
F. profunda	Pumpkin ash	450,366	—	—	—	—	450,366
Ginkgo biloba	Ginkgo, maidenhair tree	—	468,569	—	—	—	468,569
Gleditsia aquatica	Waterlocust	35,386	—	—	35,299	437,511	508,196
G. triacanthos	Honeylocust	994,729	376,157	1,319,849	35,299	5,351,919	8,077,953

continued

14

Table 1—Tree species recorded on Mississippi forest land and number of estimated live trees > 1.0 inch d.b.h., by unit and statewide (continued)

Scientific name	Common name	FIA survey unit					Statewide total
		Delta	North	Central	South	Southwest	
				number			
Gordonia lasianthus	Loblolly-bay	—	—	—	38,818	—	38,818
Gymnocladus dioicus	Kentucky coffeetree	—	—	446,198	—	—	446,198
Halesia diptera	Two-wing silverbell	35,836	—	—	923,252	1,912,155	2,871,243
H. spp.	Silverbell spp.	—	—	482,018	1,797,645	2,962,284	5,241,947
Ilex opaca	American holly	—	11,973,771	29,506,643	85,912,532	11,491,830	138,884,775
Juglans cinerea	Butternut	—	1,405,708	505,979	—	37,621	1,949,307
J. nigra	Black walnut	285,339	714,698	929,997		188,104	2,118,139
Juniperus virginiana	Eastern redcedar	9,640,849	102,714,120	28,025,384	2,362,105	9,874,503	152,616,961
Liquidambar styraciflua	Sweetgum	84,086,464	682,376,498	662,852,703	262,126,612	370,985,832	2,062,428,108
Liriodendron tulipifera	Yellow-poplar	15,588,822	149,932,716	82,339,474	56,152,902	22,226,424	326,240,338
Maclura pomifera	Osage-orange	35,836	6,101,603	2,023,089		1,142,953	9,303,482
Magnolia acuminata	Cucumbertree	628,065	37,616	—	70,597	2,999,905	3,736,183
M. fraseri	Mountain or Fraser magnolia	—	—	—	545,603	—	545,603
M. grandiflora	Southern magnolia	547,404	—	5,692,187	13,353,153	16,020,495	35,613,239
M. macrophylla	Bigleaf magnolia	1,534,703	3,505,678	593,039	35,299	9,774,280	15,442,998
M. virginiana	Sweetbay	—	3,324,108	29,795,973	202,506,016	7,322,656	242,948,752
Malus angustifolia	Southern crab apple	—	421,621	914,577	2,224,794	937,267	4,498,259
M. coronaria	Sweet crab apple	—	421,621	—	1,031,166	—	1,452,787
M. spp.	Apple spp.	—	—	—	35,299	—	35,299
Melia azedarach	Chinaberry	1,094,808		—	559,281	2,527,663	5,360,236
Morus alba	White mulberry	—	506,185	446,198	35,299	619,117	1,606,799
M. rubra	Red mulberry	2,336,767	6,585,763	4,938,085	2,272,650	5,075,921	21,209,186
Nyssa aquatica	Water tupelo	1,846,828	2,695,744	721,738	19,519,517	921,489	25,705,317
N. biflora	Swamp tupelo	35,386	2,048,428	9,397,604	61,595,019	1,554,129	74,630,567
N. ogeche	Ogeechee tupelo	—	37,616	—	38,818	—	76,434
N. sylvatica	Blackgum	4,136,147	131,867,931	142,439,970	153,888,204	48,351,272	480,683,524
Ostrya virginiana	Eastern hophornbeam	49,997,874	82,093,311	32,893,718	10,067,551	68,314,796	243,367,250
Oxydendrum arboreum	Sourwood	106,158	28,374,433	51,711,931	11,131,727	16,555,085	107,879,333
Paulownia tomentosa	Paulownia, empress-tree	587,947	112,847	—	—	33,613	734,407
Persea borbonia	Redbay	—	—	2,748,830	32,816,559	2,025,017	37,590,407
Pinus echinata	Shortleaf pine	3,181,516	99,331,855	21,896,957	24,497,911	10,559,616	159,467,855
P. elliottii	Slash pine	—	637,803	5,131,015	149,459,111	—	155,227,929
P. glabra	Spruce pine	—	—	7,898,193	6,121,761	3,130,707	17,150,662
P. palustris	Longleaf pine	—	506,185	1,991,079	54,299,552	330,572	57,127,389
P. serotina	Pond pine	—	—	—	—	33,613	33,613
P. taeda	Loblolly pine	37,864,196	704,670,109	1,034,147,053	628,105,814	591,453,497	2,996,240,669
P. virginiana	Virginia pine	—	993,705	1,963,140	1,566,211	2,737,521	7,260,577
Planera aquatica	Water elm, planertree	5,221,652	9,461,570	1,481,875	638,817	4,817,137	21,621,051
Platanus occidentalis	American sycamore	12,300,297	21,346,864	4,610,002	1,879,628	10,408,695	50,545,485
Populus deltoides	Eastern cottonwood	8,878,127	2,047,076	3,901,358	108,004	321,567	15,256,133
P. heterophylla	Swamp cottonwood	108,463		—	—	—	108,463
Prunus americana	American plum	1,327,994	2,811,415	1,784,794	918,231	1,033,902	7,876,336
P. pensylvanica	Pin cherry	—	37,616	914,577	—	—	952,193
P. serotina	Black cherry	11,540,346	126,011,785	96,463,201	62,065,629	50,408,578	346,489,539
P. virginiana	Chokecherry	440,795	—	1,873,514	—	506,254	2,820,564
Quercus alba	White oak	6,764,510	124,920,645	87,546,168	18,917,444	32,880,227	271,028,994

continued

Table 1—Tree species recorded on Mississippi forest land and number of estimated live trees > 1.0 inch d.b.h., by unit and statewide (continued)

Scientific name	Common name	FIA survey unit					Statewide total
		Delta	North	Central	South	Southwest	
				number			
Q. bicolor	Swamp white oak	—	—	—	35,299	—	35,299
Q. buckleyi	Nuttall oak	8,143,979	4,893,009	4,778,686	501,114	146,476	18,463,263
Q. coccinea	Scarlet oak	35,836	4,153,758	506,819	—	71,234	4,767,648
Q. falcata	Southern red oak	6,338,311	121,309,036	59,315,811	53,615,218	36,857,533	277,435,909
Q. imbricaria	Shingle oak	—	—	—	483,545	—	483,545
Q. incana	Bluejack oak	—	37,616	446,198	2,677,058	—	3,160,872
Q. laevis	Turkey oak	—	—	517,838	5,906,213	150,483	6,574,535
Q. laurifolia	Laurel oak	881,591	1,832,688	18,569,512	60,685,261	6,726,082	88,695,134
Q. lyrata	Overcup oak	12,906,731	2,684,641	1,936,178	5,477,809	278,429	23,283,789
Q. margarettiae	Dwarf post oak	—	—	—	888,167	—	888,167
Q. marilandica	Blackjack oak	—	6,011,369	4,735,153	7,843,248	1,661,231	20,251,001
Q. michauxii	Swamp chestnut oak	1,901,285	2,534,178	3,483,738	1,307,990	8,069,872	17,297,064
Q. muehlenbergii	Chinkapin oak	496,756	3,644,835	984,712	35,299	1,050,130	6,211,730
Q. nigra	Water oak	27,594,721	110,267,869	299,953,057	342,477,358	182,447,511	962,740,516
Q. oglethorpensis	Oglethorpe oak	—	—	35,820	—	—	35,820
Q. pagoda	Cherrybark oak	7,462,729	38,508,498	16,743,350	3,520,787	30,729,745	96,965,108
Q. palustris	Pin oak	—	468,569	35,820	—	—	504,389
Q. phellos	Willow oak	5,596,041	12,048,698	20,493,283	8,179,899	8,994,608	55,312,529
Q. prinus	Chestnut oak	—	3,676,576	—	—	33,613	3,710,189
Q. rubra	Northern red oak	689,716	16,367,126	214,919	—	409,822	17,681,583
Q. shumardii	Shumard oak	641,319	4,417,583	3,676,712	1,083,545	1,167,973	10,987,132
Q. similis	Delta post oak	142,445	—	483,799	—	37,621	663,864
Q. sinuata	Durand oak	—	75,231	3,645,871	—	—	3,721,102
Q. stellata	Post oak	1,355,844	59,023,363	30,130,640	25,350,640	9,420,033	125,280,520
Q. velutina	Black oak	4,514,171	32,771,066	13,155,723	3,003,286	4,943,404	58,387,650
Q. virginiana	Live oak	—	—	928,217	3,803,160	67,226	4,798,602
Robinia pseudoacacia	Black locust	6,360,195	6,602,643	—	35,299	3,434,530	16,432,666
Sabal palmetto	Cabbage palmetto	—	—	—	35,299	—	35,299
Salix alba	White willow	—	—	—	547,711	—	547,711
S. amygdaloides	Peachleaf willow	—	—	35,820	—	—	35,820
S. nigra	Black willow	9,329,611	48,160,901	15,744,302	6,654,171	18,232,073	98,121,058
S. sepulcralis	Weeping willow	—	—	35,067	—	—	35,067
Sassafras albidum	Sassafras	7,160,209	28,084,070	29,071,316	15,793,290	3,874,718	83,983,604
Sideroxylon lanuginosum	Chittamwood, gum bumelia	35,836	—	—	1,450,636	—	1,486,472
Taxodium ascendens	Pondcypress	—	—	—	9,652,598	—	9,652,598
T. distichum	Baldcypress	1,799,627	2,872,720	431,618	25,200,383	5,064,578	35,368,926
Tilia americana	American basswood	1,735,226	1,080,063	—	105,896	5,544,954	8,466,139
Tree unknown	Other or unknown tree	—	150,463	—	—	1,776,011	1,926,473
Triadica sebifera	Chinese tallowtree	—	3,974,248	2,632,375	32,408,122	10,196,341	49,211,085
Ulmus alata	Winged elm	42,811,775	254,704,190	113,704,245	8,767,203	99,844,335	519,831,748
U. americana	American elm	25,478,466	27,659,804	15,556,981	6,526,215	20,297,847	95,519,314
U. crassifolia	Cedar elm	3,793,799	—	517,838	141,195	—	4,452,831
U. rubra	Slippery elm	14,845,208	21,636,375	11,474,635	580,901	8,343,624	56,880,744
U. serotina	September elm	—	468,569	—	—	—	468,569
U. thomasii	Rock elm	—	—	35,820	—	—	35,820
Vernicia fordii	Tungoil tree	—	—	—	5,045,925	37,621	5,083,546

FIA = Forest Inventory and Analysis; — = no sample for the cell.

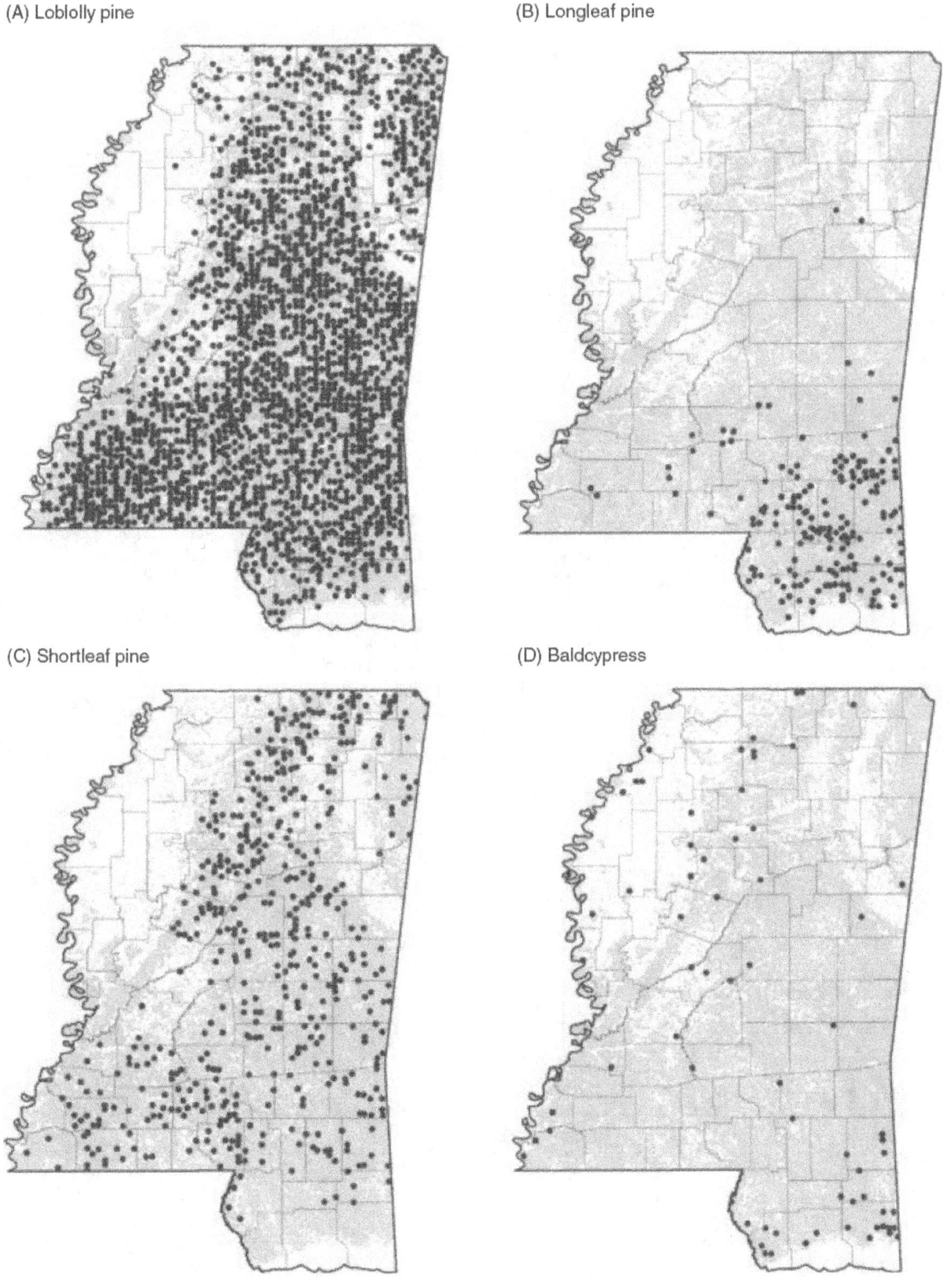

(A) Loblolly pine

(B) Longleaf pine

(C) Shortleaf pine

(D) Baldcypress

Figure 20—Distribution of four important softwoods: (A) loblolly pine, (B) longleaf pine, (C) shortleaf pine, and (D) baldcypress in Mississippi, 2006. Dots indicate the presence of the species on a given plot.

(A) Sweetgum

(B) Water oak

(C) Cherrybark oak

(D) Red maple

Figure 21—Distribution of four important hardwoods: (A) sweetgum, (B) water oak, (C) cherrybark oak, and (D) red maple in Mississippi, 2006. Dots indicate the presence of the species on a given plot.

Productive capacity refers to "the ability of a forest to provide extractive goods and services" (U.S. Department of Agriculture 2004). In Mississippi, forests are essential to the State economy; therefore, the productive capacity of the forest land is of great interest. Productive capacity can be monitored by comparing tree growth to tree removals and mortality. A positive growth-to-removal/mortality ratio indicates that the productive capacity of the forest is being maintained. A negative ratio suggests overharvesting, or it can reflect a severe insect or disease outbreak or a devastating weather event.

Timberland Area

Almost 100 percent of Mississippi's forest land is potentially available for timber production. The overwhelming majority (78 percent) of the 19.5 million acres of timberland in the State is owned by nonindustrial private forest landowners not associated with forest industry (fig. 22). Ten percent of Mississippi's timberland is owned by forest industry, while 7 percent is owned by the National Forest System and 5 percent is owned by other public entities, including State lands and other Federal lands.

Forty-six percent of the timberland area in Mississippi is occupied by sawtimber-size stands (fig. 23), an increase of about 17 percent since 1994. Twenty-seven percent of timberland area is in the sapling-seedling category, while only 1 percent is considered nonstocked. The remainder of timberland area is occupied by poletimber-size stands. Land classified as sapling-seedling has decreased by about 25 percent since the 1994 survey. Stand-size class distributions are proportioned similarly for the North, Central, and South units of Mississippi. The

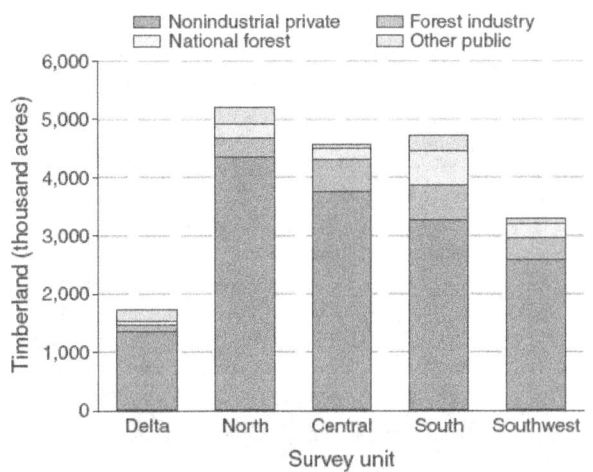

Figure 22—Timberland ownership in Mississippi by survey unit and owner class, Mississippi, 2006.

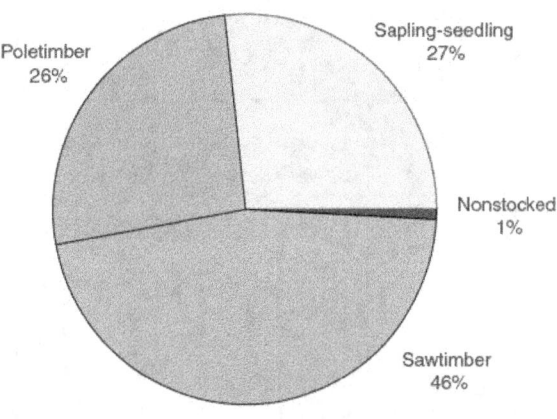

Figure 23—Area of timberland by size class, Mississippi, 2006.

Delta and Southwestern units have larger proportions of timberland area occupied by sawtimber-size stands compared to the other three units (fig. 24).

Between 1994 and 2006, most FIA units experienced declines in the area of timberland occupied by stands in the sapling-seedling size class and increases in the area of timberland occupied by stands in the poletimber and sawtimber-size classes (fig. 25). This suggests that forests that were established in the mid-1990s are recruiting into the next size class. One exception is the Delta region, where there has been an increase in the area of timberland occupied by stands primarily composed of saplings and seedlings and a decrease in the area occupied by sawtimber. The increased area of small size classes in the Delta may be a reflection of increased planting and afforestation efforts.

Volume

Live-tree volume on timberland has increased 25 percent since 1994, from 24.4 to 29.5 billion cubic feet. Live-tree volume has increased in all but the 16-inch diameter class (fig. 26). However, readers should be aware of changes in per-tree expansion factors with the switch from prism plots to fixed-radius plots. Those changes may account for some of the volume differences noted between 1994 and 2006. Trees > 22 inches d.b.h. account for about 16 percent of live-tree volume, while trees between 10 and 16 inches d.b.h. account for a combined 47 percent of the live-tree volume.

Per-acre live-tree volume increased on timberland in all units except the Delta (fig. 27). The slight per-acre volume reduction in the Delta reflects the increase in total acreage that is occupied by small-diameter stands, as mentioned previously. Even with the reduction in per-acre volume since 1994, the Delta ranks second in terms of per-area volume production. The Southwest ranks first at 1,789 cubic feet per acre.

The majority of the live-tree volume in the Delta, North, and Southwest units comes from hardwood species, while the majority of the volume in the Central and South units comes from softwood species (fig. 28). Fifty-six percent of the total live-tree volume in the State comes from hardwoods, while the remaining 44 percent is softwood volume.

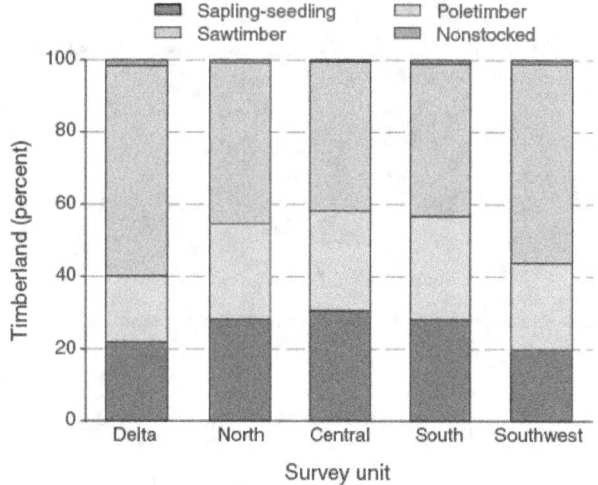

Figure 24—Proportion of acres in each survey unit by size class, Mississippi, 2006.

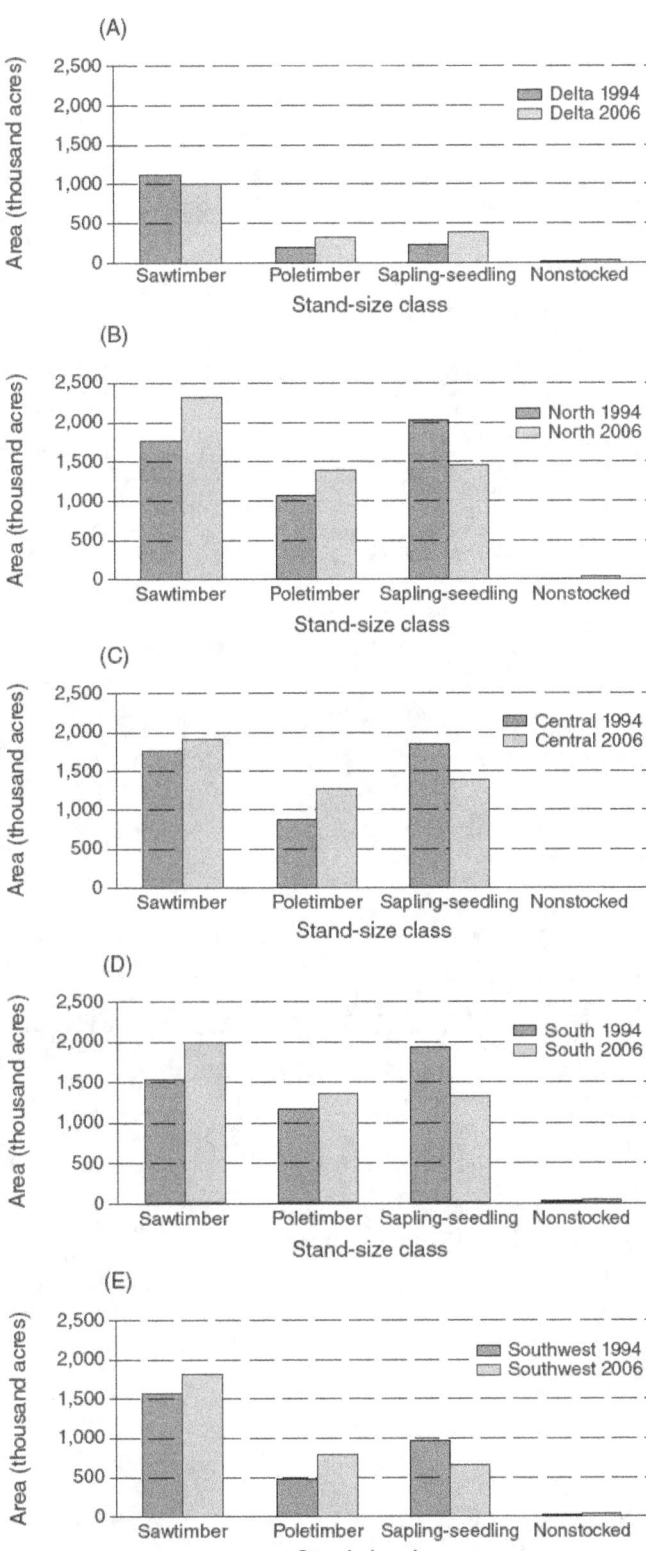

Figure 25—Area of timberland in Mississippi by survey unit: (A) Delta, (B) North, (C) Central, (D) South, and (E) Southwest; stand-size class, and year.

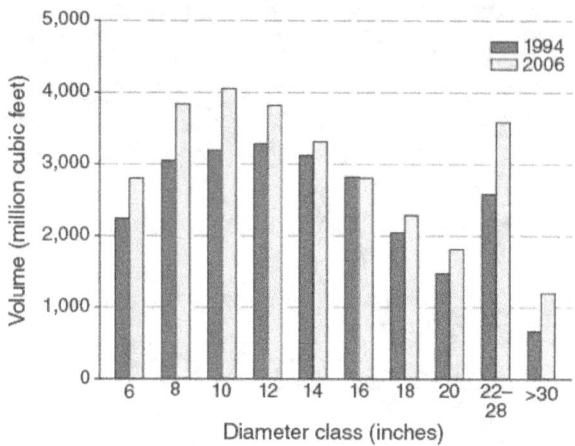

Figure 26—Volume of all live trees > 5.0 inches d.b.h. on timberland in Mississippi by survey year and diameter class.

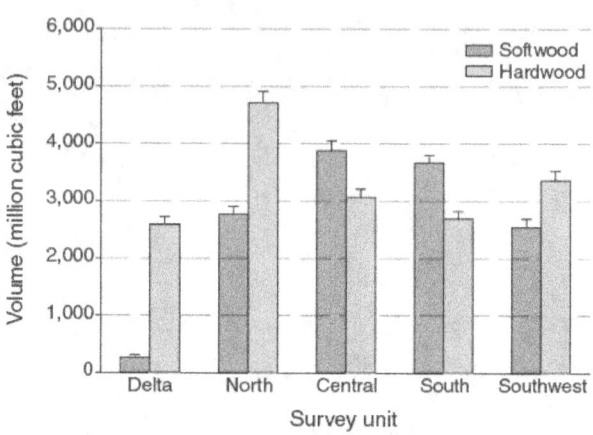

Figure 28—Live-tree volume (±one standard error) by survey unit and major species group, Mississippi, 2006.

Growth, Mortality, and Removals

Total net annual growth of live-tree volume averaged 1.4 billion cubic feet annually. Mortality averaged 344.2 million cubic feet, an increase over previous inventories that reflects, in part, losses due to Hurricanes Katrina and Ivan. Timber removals averaged 1.1 billion cubic feet, which is 4 percent of the current timberland inventory.

Average net annual live-tree timber removals rose steadily from the 1970s through the 1990s, and even surpassed growth in the 1994 inventory. The 2006 inventory shows a decrease in net annual live-tree removals, ending the trend and resulting in a positive growth-to-removal ratio (fig. 29). Net annual live-tree growth has increased steadily since the late 1970s.

Softwood net annual removals surpassed net annual growth in 1994, suggesting overharvesting during that time period. However, that trend appears to have reversed between the 1994 inventory and the current inventory. Now, softwood growth exceeds removals by 29 percent. Similarly, while hardwood net annual removals exceeded growth in 1994, net annual hardwood growth now exceeds removals by 22 percent (fig. 30).

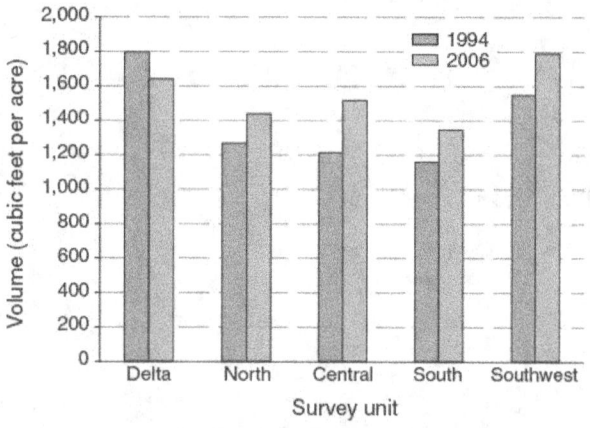

Figure 27—Live-tree volume on timberland in Mississippi by survey year and survey unit.

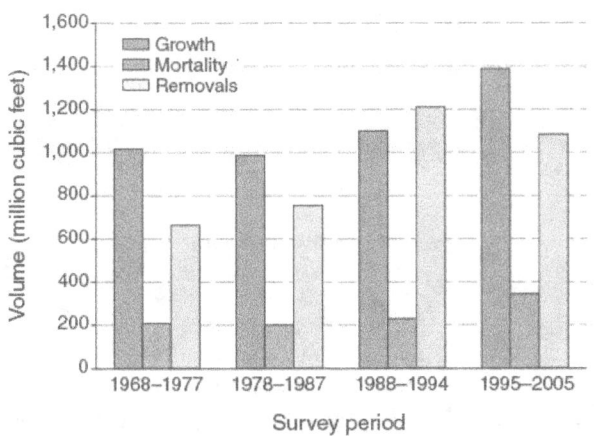

Figure 29—Average net annual growth, mortality, and removals of all live trees on timberland in Mississippi by survey period.

Cherrybark oak log sections in Mississippi. (photo by Christopher M. Oswalt)

(A)

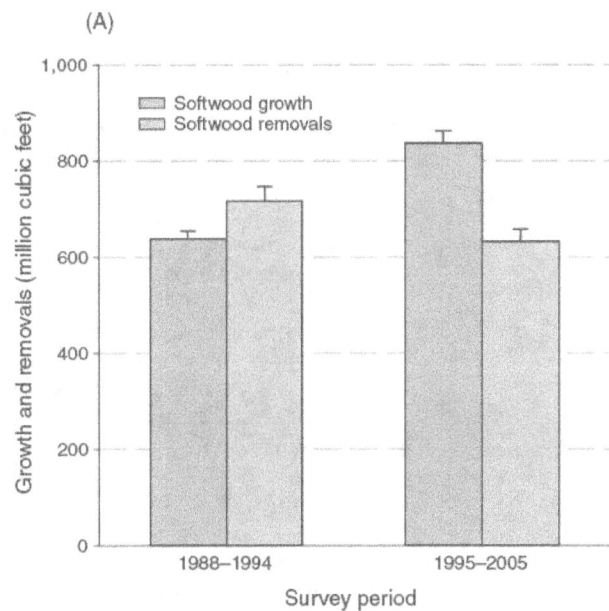

(B)

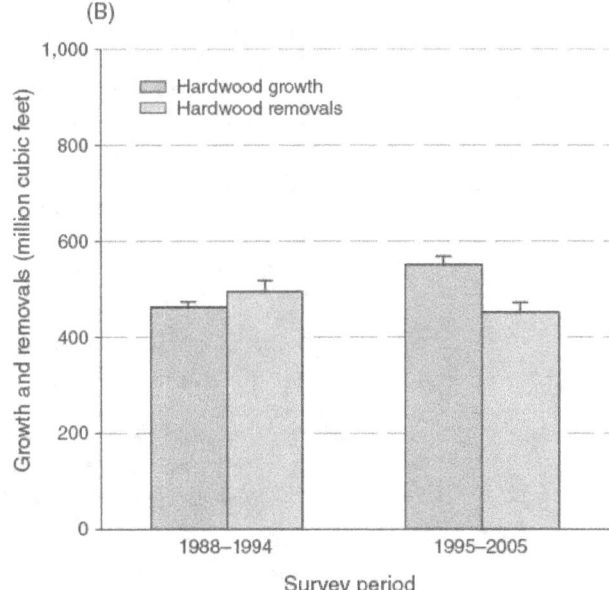

Figure 30—Average annual growth and removals (±one standard error) of live trees by survey period and major species group: (A) softwood and (B) hardwood.

The concept of forest health relates to the ability of a system to continue to provide ecological functions and values for the various organisms that dwell within the system. When the health of the forest is threatened or compromised, so are the organisms that depend on the forest, including humans. Disturbances that affect substantial areas of forest land have the potential to change developmental pathways, alter species composition, and modify the functional capacity of the forest. Estimates of levels of invasive plants, insects, and diseases provide some insight into the condition of Mississippi's forest resources.

Nonnative Invasive Plant Species

Nonnative invasive plants are a threat to many forests in the South and across the Nation. Invasive plants can displace native species, alter the physical and chemical properties of the soil, and result in decreased tree regeneration by shading the forest floor (Oswalt and others 2007), which can impact the ecological and economic trajectories of forest stands. In Mississippi, 13,418 forested subplots were surveyed for up to 4 nonnative invasive plants selected from a list of species known to be problematic in Southern States (U.S. Department of Agriculture 2005).

Japanese honeysuckle was the most frequently recorded invasive plant species on Mississippi forests, with observations on 7,124 subplots. Nonnative privet (*Ligustrum* sp.) and Japanese climbing fern (*Lygodium japonicum*) were the next most

commonly recorded species, with records on 3,524 and 869 subplots, respectively. The distribution of these and two other species of particular concern in Mississippi is given in figure 31. Other well-known invasive plants less frequently recorded on subplots were Chinese tallowtree (*Triadica sebifera*; fig. 30), cogongrass (*Imperata cylindrical*; fig. 31), and kudzu (*Peuraria Montana*; not shown). The reason for this is that a widely distributed, systematic plot network is not a sensitive tool for detecting scattered, clustered, or linear distributions often represented by these advancing species. These plants are, in fact, fairly common and widespread in Mississippi and, especially in the case of cogongrass, spreading rapidly. Cogongrass, in particular, poses a greater threat to forest ecosystems than other more common invasive plants such as Japanese honeysuckle, and is known to occur in most Mississippi counties (http://www.seeppc.org/eddMapS/statedist.cfm?sub=2433&id=us_ms).

Insects and Diseases

Common diseases and insects currently affecting Mississippi's forest resources are summarized in table 2 (Eastern Forest Environmental Threat Assessment Center 2007). Of those, southern pine beetle (SPB) (*Dendroctonus frontalis*) and pine engraver beetles (*Ips grandicollis, I. calligraphus, I. avulses*) are among the most devastating insect species in Mississippi's important softwood resource (Eastern Forest Environmental Threat Assessment Center 2007, Mississippi Forestry Commission 2006). The SPB has affected much of

Tree frog clinging to Japanese honeysuckle vine on Noxubee Refuge, Mississippi. (photo by Christoper M. Oswalt)

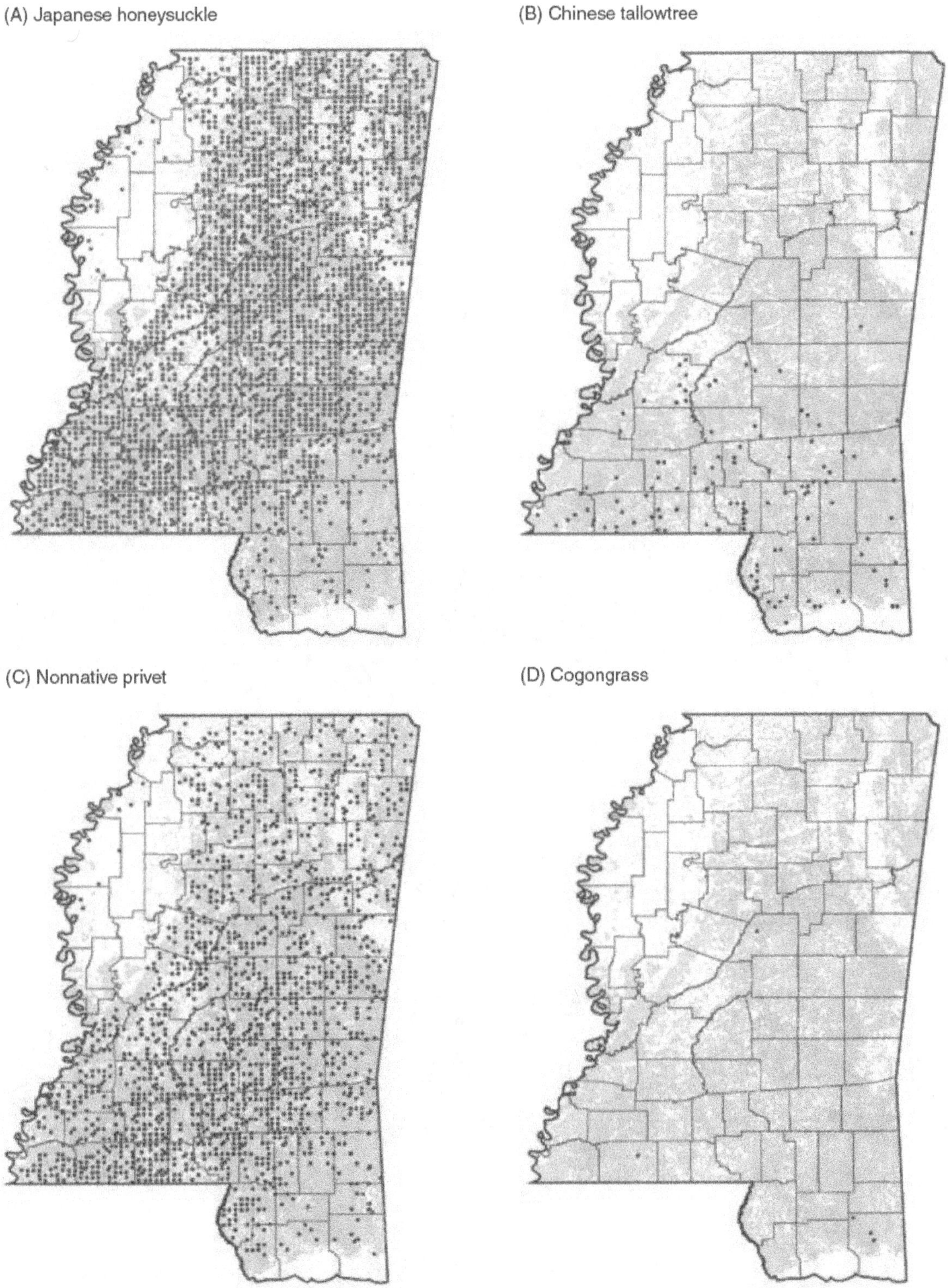

(A) Japanese honeysuckle

(B) Chinese tallowtree

(C) Nonnative privet

(D) Cogongrass

Figure 31—Distribution of four invasive species: (A) Japanese honeysuckle, (B) Chinese tallowtree, (C) nonnative privet, and (D) cogongrass of concern on Mississippi's forests, as collected on FIA forested sample plots (data courtesy Samuel Lambert, U.S. Forest Service, Southern Research Station, FIA).

the Southern United States in the last 60 years, and has continued to impact Mississippi's forests since the 1994 forest inventory. In fact, Mississippi experienced a large outbreak of SPB in 1995, when 24 counties were in outbreak status (Pye and others 2004; fig. 32). That outbreak alone caused over $16 million in damages (Pye and others 2004; fig. 33). Since that large outbreak, SPB infestations have generally been at low levels across the State, with occasional and localized areas of moderate-to-high infestation levels associated with some of the national forests. However, the risk for a large SPB epidemic still exists and

Table 2—Diseases and insects currently threatening Mississippi's forests

Common name	Scientific name	Comments
Diseases		
Annosus root disease	*Heterobasidion annosum*	Root rotting fungus that causes pockets of mortality after thinning in pine stands.
Armillaria root disease	*Armillaria mellea, A. tabescens, A. gallica*	Root rotting fungus that affects primarily hardwood trees contributing to mortality as in oak decline events.
Fusiform rust	*Cronartium quercuum f. sp. fusiforme*	Canker-causing fungus which can cause devastating losses to young pine plantations.
Pitch canker	*Fusarium circinatum*	Canker-causing fungus which causes shoot and limb dieback in young pine plantations, seed orchards, and nursery beds.
Oak decline	Various	Syndrome caused by predisposing, inciting, and secondary factors resulting in dieback and mortality of oak species.
Insects		
Pine engraver beetles	*Ips grandicollis, I. calligraphus, I. avulsus*	Bark beetles which kill branches, tops, and trees that have been stressed, weakened, and/or damaged by drought, fire, storms, etc.
Black turpentine beetle	*Dendroctonus terebrans*	Large pine bark beetle that typically attacks the base of older larger trees and is capable of causing tree mortality.
Nantucket pine tip moth	*Rhyacionia frustrana*	Lepidopteran whose larvae bore into the tips of terminals and lateral branches causing dieback, growth loss, and deformity in young loblolly pine.
Regeneration weevils	*Hylobius pales* and *Pachylobius picivorus*	Weevils whose adult feeding on shoots of young pine seedlings can girdle and kill seedlings, causing potential planting failures.
Southern pine beetle	*Dendroctonus frontalis*	A tree-killing bark beetle which exhibits periodic outbreaks causing rapid and widespread tree mortality.
Twolined chestnut borer	*Agrilus bilineatus*	Flat headed borer often responsible for girdling of oaks; often associated with oak decline.
Red oak borer	*Enaphalodes rufulus*	Round headed borer usually causing lumber degrade but recently associated with oak decline events.

Source: Eastern Forest Environmental Threat Assessment Center (2007).

large areas of pine forest are susceptible to infestation and damage. Also, even when counties do not reach outbreak status, smaller diffuse infestations may occur, resulting in economic impacts statewide. For example, SPB reached outbreak status in 1996 in 11 counties, but the economic damage to the State was less than that in 1998, when no counties reached outbreak status (figs. 32 and 33). In 1998, however, a larger number of spots were reported, but were spread over a larger number of counties. Since outbreak status is determined by density of infestation spots, no counties reached outbreak status, but the economic damage was substantial, nonetheless (Personal communication. 2008. John Pye, Ecologist, Southern Research Station, Forest Economics and Policy, P.O. Box 12254, Research Triangle Park, NC 27709).

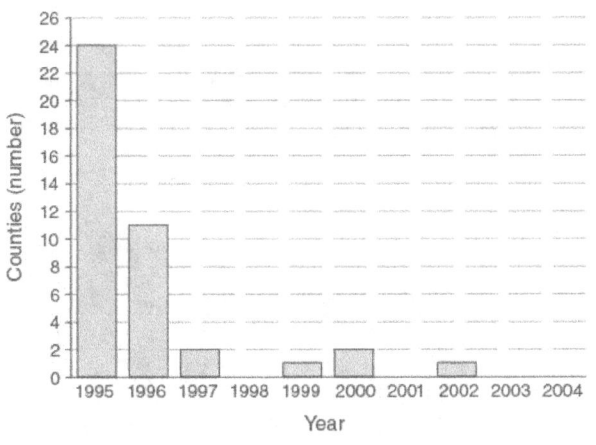

Figure 32—Number of Mississippi counties with southern pine beetle outbreaks, 1995 to 2004 (Pye and others 2004).

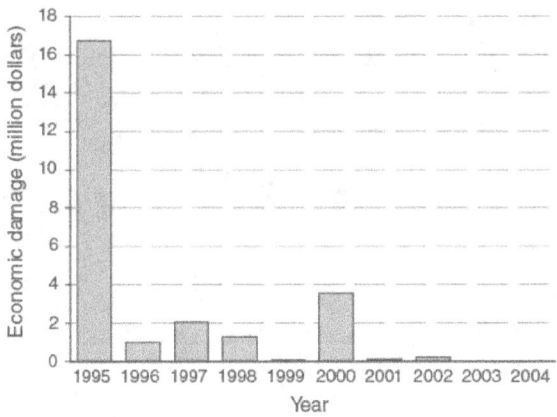

Figure 33—Annual economic damage (adjusted for inflation to 2004) in Mississippi as a result of southern pine beetle outbreaks, 1995 to 2004 (Pye and others 2004).

Silkworm infestation on the Natchez trace. (photo by Sonja N. Oswalt)

Forest Inventory and Analysis cruiser measures the diameter of a tree in Mississippi. (photo by Andrew Edwards, U.S. Forest Service)

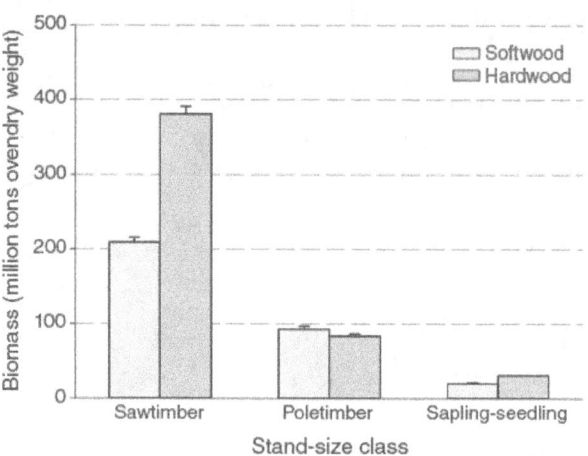

Figure 34—All live biomass on forest land (±one standard error) in Mississippi by major species group and stand-size class, 2006.

Increasing interest in global climate change and carbon dioxide produced through industrial and vehicular emissions has led to a parallel interest in the ability of forests to sequester carbon. Carbon sequestration, the ability of living material to capture carbon from the atmosphere, thereby offsetting carbon produced by emissions from combustibles, is now receiving much attention in the scientific community (Johnsen and others 2001). The concept of carbon sequestration directly impacts the global economy, surfacing in the political and economic realm in the form of carbon credits and carbon trading in the stock market. A forest ecosystem can be either a source of carbon dioxide in the atmosphere (through respiration, decomposition, harvest, fire, insect or disease defoliation) or a sink of carbon dioxide (by fixing carbon into living biomass through photosynthesis). Net changes in forest carbon stocks help to identify whether a forest ecosystem is a carbon source or sink.

Forest Biomass and Carbon

Forest biomass is the living material present in a forest ecosystem, and is also a useful measure of tree and forest productivity. Biomass estimates provide information about a species' ability to collect nutrients and other resources, offering managers another measure of a species' influence within a particular forest community (Spetich and Parker 1998). The carbon contained in trees can be assumed to be roughly 50 percent of the measured biomass (dry weight) of the tree (Nabuurs and others 2004). Furthermore, per-acre carbon dioxide uptake may be estimated by multiplying the carbon content of the tree by the value 3.67 (mass conversion factor; Clark 1982).

In 2006, aboveground biomass (dry weight) for Mississippi's forest land averaged 42 tons per acre, or 816.7 million tons, statewide. Merchantable biomass accounted for 72 percent of statewide biomass. Hardwood trees contribute over one-half of the aboveground biomass in Mississippi's forests, and most of that comes from sawtimber-size stands with large average diameters (fig. 34). Using the above conversions, about 77 tons of carbon dioxide is

sequestered in an acre of Mississippi forest land. In other words, burning 1 acre of forest in Mississippi would release about 77 tons of CO_2 into the atmosphere.

Mississippi's forests provide more than just environmental benefits to the people of the State; they also provide economic and social benefits through goods and services. Wood products, nontimber forest products (NTFP), and forest-related recreation, e.g., tourism, hunting, fishing, and wildlife viewing, all contribute to the development of Mississippi's economy.

Timber Product Output

Timber product and the economy—
The forest products industry in Mississippi is very diverse, ranging from small and medium-size hardwood sawmills to very large softwood sawmills, pulpmills, and plywood mills. Mississippi's forest products industry is a vital component of the State's

economy, with timber ranking as the second most valuable agricultural product. Mississippi State University Extension Service severance tax data showed that Mississippi landowners received $10.8 billion for their standing timber between 1995 and 2006, or nearly $899 million annually. The value of timber delivered to mills averaged $1.22 billion over the same time period. Table 3 shows the value of standing and delivered timber by individual years and species group (Mississippi State University, Cooperative Extension Service 1996, 1997, 1998, 1999, 2000, 2001, 2002, 2003, 2004, 2005, 2006).

In 2005, about 103 sawmills, pulpwood mills, and other primary wood-processing plants distributed across the State (fig. 35) directly employed nearly 18,000 individuals, with an annual payroll of $685 million. In 2005, the combined value of shipments for the wood products and paper manufacturing sectors was about

Table 3—Value of standing and delivered timber by individual year and species group, 1995–2006[a]

	Value of standing timber			Value of delivered timber		
Year	Softwood	Hardwood	Total	Softwood	Hardwood	Total
			dollars			
1995	613,862,197	152,755,959	766,618,156	807,508,765	291,178,385	1,098,687,150
1996	706,043,908	171,838,012	877,881,920	889,202,254	292,728,039	1,181,930,293
1997	821,247,557	202,980,999	1,024,228,556	1,006,033,708	299,689,154	1,305,722,862
1998	848,326,473	237,424,852	1,085,751,325	1,019,445,944	333,270,090	1,352,716,034
1999	820,132,005	198,302,961	1,018,434,966	957,184,579	296,936,326	1,254,120,905
2000	800,180,193	197,440,695	997,620,888	997,296,731	300,484,879	1,297,781,610
2001	643,859,855	153,211,124	797,070,979	829,468,714	240,935,666	1,070,404,380
2002	659,363,608	121,744,306	781,107,914	840,351,497	193,932,200	1,034,283,697
2003	647,991,282	160,125,294	808,116,576	855,914,699	239,187,829	1,095,102,528
2004	693,828,262	166,047,277	859,875,539	991,680,537	264,294,483	1,255,975,020
2005	785,845,249	157,178,802	943,024,051	1,123,364,892	322,470,332	1,445,835,224
2006	701,469,996	123,229,597	824,699,593	965,944,013	237,201,956	1,203,145,969
Total	8,742,150,585	2,042,279,878	10,784,430,463	11,283,396,333	3,312,309,339	14,595,705,672
Average	728,512,549	170,189,990	898,702,539	940,283,028	276,025,778	1,216,308,806

[a] Data from Mississippi State University Cooperative Extension Service, 1995–2006.

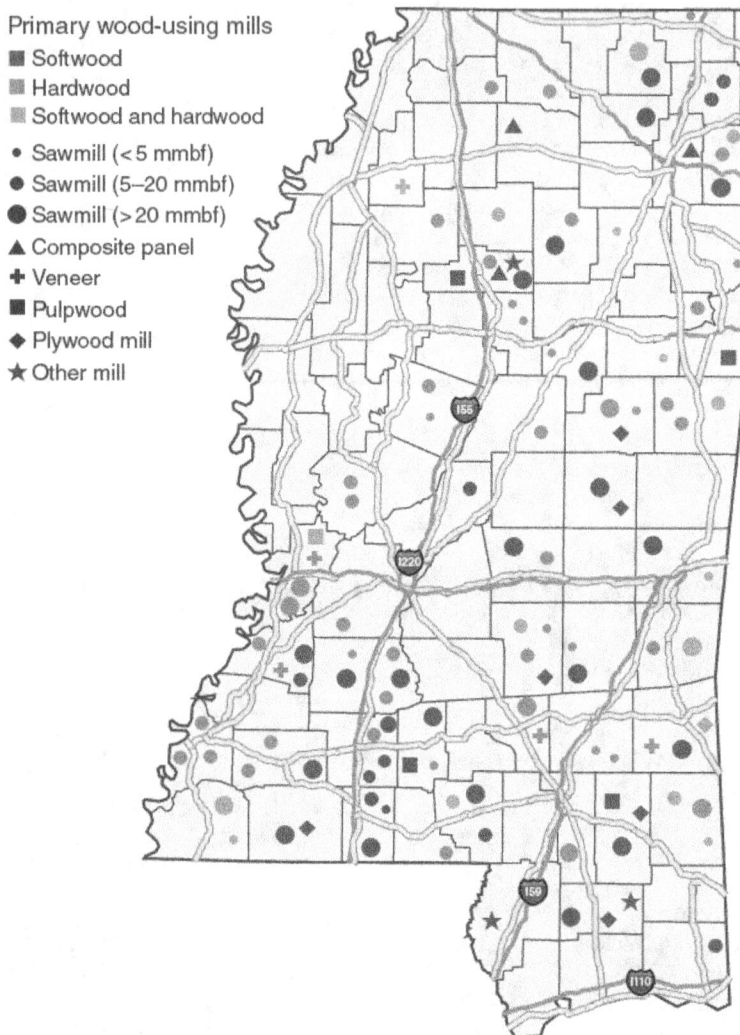

Primary wood-using mills

■ Softwood
▨ Hardwood
▨ Softwood and hardwood

• Sawmill (< 5 mmbf)
● Sawmill (5–20 mmbf)
● Sawmill (> 20 mmbf)
▲ Composite panel
✚ Veneer
■ Pulpwood
◆ Plywood mill
★ Other mill

Figure 35—Primary wood-using mills in Mississippi by mill type, wood type, and major interstate roads. (Road information courtesy ESRI)

$2.24 billion (U.S. Department of Commerce 2005). Table 4 shows employment, payroll, and value of shipments for Mississippi forest products for the years 1997 through 2005. The number of employees fluctuated from > 26,500 in 1997 to 17,971 in 2005, and averaged 22,190 employees over the time period. The payroll for the same time period averaged $726 million, reaching a peak of $792 million in 1998. Values of shipments have remained relatively stable over those years, and averaged $2.22 billion for the time period. According to IMpact Analysis for PLANning (IMPLAN), a model generated by the Forest Service (Abt and others 2002), the total economic importance of Mississippi's forests in 2001 was calculated to be nearly $10.9 billion. This dollar value represents all activities associated with the forest products industry, including direct, indirect, and induced effects resulting from the industry operation.

Timber product output and removals—
Estimates of timber product output (TPO) and plant residues for the period 1995 through 2006 were obtained from questionnaires sent to all major primary wood-using mills in the State. The questionnaires were used to determine the types and amount of roundwood, i.e., saw logs, pulpwood, plywood and veneer, poles, etc., received by each mill, the county of origin of the wood, the species used, and how the mills disposed of the bark and wood residues produced. The questionnaires were conducted every 3 to 4 years by personnel from the Southern Research Station and the Mississippi Forestry Commission. These data are used to augment FIA's annual inventory of timber removals by providing the proportions by product for the segment of removals that

Table 4—Bureau of the Census statistics for Mississippi forest products, 1997–2005

Year	Employees	Payroll	Value of shipments
	number	thousand dollars	
1997	26,530	789,487	2,293,318
1998	25,797	791,589	2,273,205
1999	25,882	784,363	2,358,679
2000	24,834	773,845	2,323,507
2001	23,395	721,629	2,007,225
2002	20,212	703,266	1,915,023
2003	17,982	644,786	2,135,380
2004	17,103	636,391	2,401,662
2005	17,971	685,016	2,244,411
Average	22,190	725,597	2,216,934

Source: U.S. Department of Commerce, Bureau of the Census (2005).

is used. Individual studies are necessary to track trends and changes in product output levels. Industry surveys conducted in 1995, 1999, 2002, and 2005 were used to determine average annual product output for roundwood and plant byproducts for the latest survey period (Bentley and others 2008, Bentley and others 2002, Howell and others 2005, Stratton and others 1998). In addition, severance tax data collected on an annual basis from 1995 to 2006 by the Mississippi State University Extension Service were used to augment the industry surveys. Therefore, volumes reported for individual products are an average value per year and will not match specific year values or reports where all years are reported. Total product output, averaged over the survey period, is the sum of the volume of roundwood products from all sources (growing stock and other sources) and the volume of plant byproducts (mill residues).

Chipmill operation in Mississippi. (photo by Sonja N. Oswalt)

Total output of timber products, which includes domestic fuelwood and plant byproducts, averaged nearly 1.17 billion cubic feet per year between 1995 and 2006. Eighty-four percent, or 983 million cubic feet, of the total output was from roundwood products, while the remainder was from plant byproducts (mill residue). At 829 million cubic feet, softwood species provided 71 percent of the total product output volume. Hardwoods provided the remaining 29 percent, or 337 million cubic feet of total output.

The number of pulpmills operating in Mississippi declined from seven in 1995 to five in 2005. However, output from these mills made pulpwood the primary wood product produced in Mississippi mills during the latest survey period. Pulpwood production averaged nearly 509 million cubic feet between 1995 and 2006, accounting for 44 percent of total product output for the State. Softwood pulpwood production totaled 319 million cubic feet and accounted for 63 percent of total pulpwood production, while hardwood pulpwood production amounted to 190 million cubic feet. Plant byproducts, or mill residue, accounted for 34 and 12 percent, respectively, of total softwood and hardwood pulpwood production. The 131 million cubic feet of plant byproducts used for pulpwood production accounted for 35 percent of mill residue utilized for products.

Saw-log production, used mainly for dimension lumber, totaled nearly 472 million cubic feet. Saw-log output, from about 93 sawmills, accounted for 40 percent of the total TPO volume between 1995 and 2006. Veneer-log production totaled 69.5 million cubic feet, while composite panel production amounted to 39 million cubic feet. Veneer and composite panel production combined accounted for 9 percent of the total product output.

At 46 million cubic feet, other industrial products (including poles) accounted for 4 percent of total product output. Industrial products accounted for 97 percent of the State's total product output. Domestic fuelwood totaled nearly 31 million cubic feet and accounted for 3 percent of total

Chipmill operation in Mississippi.
(photo by Sonja N. Oswalt)

product output for the State. Mill residue used for industrial fuel amounted to 190 million cubic feet and accounted for 51 percent of the total mill byproducts utilized.

Figure 36 shows trends in average annual roundwood product output from 1948 through 2006. While roundwood used for saw logs and other industrial products was up slightly, roundwood used for veneer logs, pulpwood, and fuelwood was down from the previous survey period. Average annual output of roundwood products (including domestic fuelwood) was down 3 percent, or 33 million cubic feet, from 1.02 billion cubic feet in the previous survey period to an average of 983 million cubic feet between 1995 and 2006. Softwood roundwood production was down 1 percent from 684 to 675 million cubic feet, while hardwood roundwood production declined 7 percent from 332 to 308 million cubic feet.

During the latest survey period, roundwood harvested for saw-log and pulpwood production amounted to 466 and 378 million cubic feet, respectively. These two products accounted for 86 percent of the total roundwood production for the State. Eighty-six percent of the roundwood products volume came from growing-stock trees, split between sawtimber (73 percent) and poletimber (27 percent). Volume from other sources, which includes premerchantable, rough cull, and salvable dead trees, and stumps and tops of harvested trees, amounted to 135 million cubic feet. This volume accounted

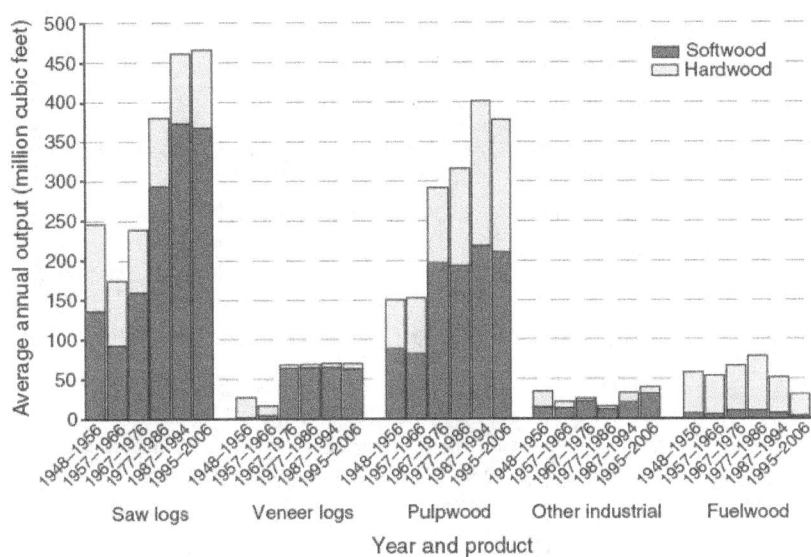

Figure 36—Average annual output of roundwood timber products by product and species group, Mississippi, 1948 to 2006.

for 14 percent of roundwood product output, which is higher than normally seen. However, about 40 percent of this volume is attributable to the salvage efforts following Hurricane Katrina. As further evidence of the effect of this powerful storm, national forest cut and sold records showed that harvest from national forests in Mississippi jumped from 12 million cubic feet in 2005 to > 58 million cubic feet in 2006. The 2006 harvest level accounted for 45 percent of the total volume harvested and 37 percent of the total timber value from all national forests in the southern region.

Total timber removals, averaged over the time period, are the sum of the volume of roundwood products, logging residues

(unused portions of trees left in the woods which includes volume from tops, limbs, and stumps), and other removals (removals attributed to land clearing or land use changes) from growing-stock and nongrowing-stock sources. Removals from all sources, for both softwoods and hardwoods combined, totaled 1.4 billion cubic feet (39.3 million tons). Softwoods accounted for 58 percent of total removals. Volume used for roundwood products totaled 983 million cubic feet (31.7 million tons or 73 percent) of total removals. Logging residues and other removals amounted to 263 million cubic feet (4.2 million tons or 19 percent) and 105 million cubic feet (3.4 million tons or 8 percent), respectively.

Nontimber Forest Products

Specialty NTFPs, recreation, water, wildlife habitat, and esthetic values contribute immensely to the State's economy and the well-being of the general population. Specialty forest products or NTFPs have been harvested from Mississippi forests for many years. Although these products contribute a much smaller percentage to the overall economy than traditional

forest products, they are nonetheless very important and provide millions of dollars to many local rural economies each year. Many of these products are collected with very little forest disturbance and range from edible products (fruits, nuts, mushrooms, ramps, and maple syrup) to medicinal products (saw palmetto and bloodroot); to ornamental products (galax, pine tips for garlands, and grapevines); to landscape products (pine straw and native plants) and specialty woods (burl and crotch wood for fine crafts).

According to a survey of county extension agents as of April 2003, Mississippi had a total of 900 NTFP enterprises (Chamberlain and Predny 2003). Table 5 shows the total number and distribution of NTFP enterprises Southwide. Forty-nine percent, or 444 of the NTFP enterprises in the State, fell into the specialty wood and landscape categories. Medicinal plants and edible products comprised 249 (28 percent) of the NTFP enterprises, while the floral and decorative products category comprised 207 (23 percent) of the firms. Mississippi ranked 10th in total number of NTFP enterprises in the southern region, accounting for 4 percent of the total NTFP firms.

Table 5—Total number and distribution of nontimber forest product enterprises in the Southern United States as perceived by county extension agents

State	Edible	Specialty wood	Floral and decorative	Landscape	Medicinal	Total
			number			
Alabama	221	377	378	377	58	1,411
Arkansas	224	257	208	120	251	1,060
Florida	216	127	182	837	50	1,412
Georgia	250	186	384	1,086	68	1,974
Kentucky	490	826	562	373	2,670	4,921
Louisiana	249	119	94	81	8	551
Mississippi	234	252	207	192	15	900
North Carolina	526	452	3,283	1,326	770	6,357
Oklahoma	275	148	75	65	14	577
South Carolina	89	81	145	216	25	556
Tennessee	390	794	481	593	314	2,572
Texas	438	210	200	196	27	1,071
Virginia	239	370	698	376	262	1,945
Total	3,841	4,199	6,897	5,838	4,532	25,307

White tailed deer fawn tucked away in the grass. (photo by W. J. Berg, U.S. Fish and Wildlife Service)

Ownership, Use, and Recreation— Results from the National Woodland Owner Survey

The primary focus of the National Woodland Owner Survey (NWOS) is private forest landowners (Butler 2008). Private ownerships, as defined by Butler (2008), are all owners other than Federal, State, and local governments. Family and individual owners (referred to as family forest owners) are defined as individual or joint ownerships that have a legally binding interest in ownership of forest land, including family or individual estates and trusts (Butler 2008). The focus of this section is on family forest owners.

The majority of Mississippi's forest land is in private hands (table 6), of which 70 percent are family forests. Results

Table 6—Area of forest land in Mississippi by ownership category, 2006

Ownership category	Area	
	Acres	SE
	thousand	*percent*
Private		
Family	12,146	1.4
Other private	5,174	2.8
Total	17,320	1.3
Public		
Federal	1,834	4.6
State	236	13.3
Local	233	13.6
Total	2,303	4.2
Total	19,622	1.3

SE = sampling error.

from the NWOS show that there are an estimated 163,000 family forest landowners in Mississippi (table 7). A large number of family forest land holdings are 100 percent forested (table 8). The majority of family forest holdings (69 percent) are at the least 75 percent forested.

The likelihood that a given tract of private forest land is managed depends on a wide variety of factors, including the number of acres owned and the reasons for owning the land. Most private family forest landowners in Mississippi have relatively small holdings. In fact, 83 percent of the State's family owned forest land is estimated to be in parcels of < 100 acres (table 7), and 53 percent are in parcels of < 20 acres. In general, harvesting costs per unit area increase as the size of landholdings decline. Large landholdings (100+ acres) can reasonably be assumed to be available for timber harvesting, but only 29,000 (17 percent) of Mississippi's 163,000 private family forest land ownerships fall in this category. Opportunities for harvesting

diminish to the point where forested parcels below a given-size threshold typically are not considered viable for commercial forestry activities. In that regard, the family owned forest ownerships estimated to be in parcels of < 10 acres are likely to be inaccessible for sustained timber production.

The great majority of Mississippi family forest ownerships have tenure of ≥ 10 years (table 9). While about 28 percent of survey respondents, accounting for an estimated 46,000 ownerships, did not indicate how long their forest had been in their ownership, 72 percent of survey respondents, accounting for an estimated 117,000 ownerships, did answer. Of those that supplied tenure information, 32 percent indicated they had owned their land between 10 and 24 years. Ten percent of family forest ownerships have a tenure > 50 years (table 9), a proportion much higher than reported in neighboring States like Tennessee, where only 2 percent of respondents indicated tenure of > 50 years (Oswalt and others 2009).

Table 7—Number of family-owned forests in Mississippi by size of forest landholding, 2006

| Size of forest landholding | Owners | |
| | Number | SE |
acres	thousand	percent
1–9	41	44.6
10–19	45	31.2
20–49	26	28.7
50–99	23	9.6
100–199	15	17.9
200–499	10	14.6
500–999	2	24.3
1,000–4,999	2	16.3
5,000–9,999	<1	53.2
10,000+	<1	51.8
Total	163	4.0

SE = sampling error.

Table 8—Number of family-owned forests in Mississippi by percent of owner's land that is forested, 2006

| Forested | Owners | |
| | Number | SE |
percent	thousand	percent
<25	5	86.8
25–49	8	57.8
50–74	37	54.7
75–99	43	32.9
100	69	36.5
No answer	<1	100.0

SE = sampling error.

Table 9—Number of family-owned forests in Mississippi by ownership tenure, 2006

| Land tenure | Owners | |
| | Number | SE |
years	thousand	percent
<10	4	47.5
10–24	37	33.6
25–49	64	27.7
50+	12	37.2
No answer	46	34.0

SE = sampling error.

The widely varied values and attitudes of family forest landowners are reflected in the reasons they give for owning their forest land. Owning land to pass along to children or other heirs was chosen by more landowners (an estimated 114,000 ownerships) as the most important objective they had for owning forest land, followed by investment (94,000), beauty and scenery enjoyment (93,000), and nature protection and biodiversity (83,000) (table 10). Recreation (hunting and other recreation) was ranked high with an estimated 91,000 family forest landowners. An estimated 60,000 owners indicated that timber production was an important reason for forest land ownership. These categories are not exclusive, meaning that those listing aesthetics (beauty and scenery enjoyment) as their most important reason for ownership are not necessarily averse to timber harvesting. In fact, many list timber harvest or other forestry activity as a recent event on their land.

According to the NWOS, timber harvests have occurred on an estimated 104,000 of Mississippi's family forest ownerships, with harvest occurring on about 28,000 ownerships within the past 5 years (tables 11 and 12). Seventy-two percent considered their timber harvest a commercial harvest (table 11). For the most part, saw logs and pulpwood were the largest product classes harvested from Mississippi family forest land ownerships (table 11). Other activities related to timber management occurring in the past 5 years include tree planting by an estimated 28,000 ownerships, and road/trail maintenance by 25,000 ownerships (table 12). Recent efforts to reduce fire hazards occurred on about 25,000 ownerships (table 12). Recreation was another major forestry activity enjoyed by many of the State's family forest landowners. Some 50,000 owners listed recreation (public and private) as an activity occurring in the past 5 years on their forest land.

Table 10—Number of family-owned forests in Mississippi by reason for owning forest land, 2006

Reason[a]	Owners	
	Number	SE
	thousand	*percent*
To enjoy beauty or scenery	93	18.5
To protect nature and biologic diversity	83	22.2
For land investment	94	18.6
Part of home or vacation home	77	36.0
Part of farm or ranch	43	49.5
Privacy	75	23.8
To pass land on to children or other heirs	114	16.6
To cultivate/collect nontimber forest products	20	41.4
For production of firewood or biofuel	9	32.6
For production of saw logs, pulpwood, or other timber products	60	18.1
Hunting or fishing	57	22.7
For recreation other than hunting or fishing	34	33.0
No answer	4	87.7

Numbers include landowners who ranked each objective as very important (1) or important (2) on a seven-point Likert scale.

SE = sampling error.

[a] Categories are not exclusive.

Table 11—Area and number of family-owned forests in Mississippi by timber harvesting activities and reasons for harvest, 2006

Family-owned forests	Area		Owners	
	Acres	SE	Number	SE
	thousand	*percent*	*thousand*	*percent*
Trees harvested or removed				
Yes	10,223	3.6	104	16.7
No	1,618	21.8	52	30.8
No answer	305	68.2	7	63.2
Products harvested[a]				
Saw logs	8,243	5.5	58	15.2
Veneer logs	2,026	28.4	8	68.1
Pulpwood	7,446	6.3	52	21.1
Firewood	2,085	18.1	15	30.1
Posts or poles	1,933	29.5	1	33.0
Other	131	121.7	<1	92.8
No answer	1,210	26.6	35	38.4
Received professional consultation[b]				
Yes	6,414	7.4	36	16.6
No	3,139	13.7	40	28.9
Uncertain	58	170.8	1	100.1
No answer	612	43.1	27	48.0
Recent harvest/removal (within 5 years)				
Yes	5,883	8.4	28	19.8
No	5,244	9.4	105	19.3
Uncertain	188	102.7	1	61.1
No answer	831	35.7	29	48.7
Commercial harvest[c]				
Yes	9,260	4.6	75	16.6
No	1,675	21.3	52	30.4
No answer	1,210	26.6	35	38.4
Reason for harvest[b]				
Part of management plan	5,066	9.7	24	25.8
Trees were mature	6,249	8.1	47	19.8
Clear land	543	44.2	16	70.0
Needed money	2,677	15.6	16	24.2
Wood for personal use	1,282	26.7	11	41.8
Price was right	3,002	14.8	24	33.2
Improve hunting	776	35.2	2	57.3
Improve recreation	236	79.3	4	98.4
Remove trees damaged by natural catastrophes	3,155	14.5	18	32.7
Improve quality of remaining trees	4,973	10.0	25	23.3
Other	438	57.6	5	53.8
No answer	856	35.4	35	42.4

SE = sampling error.

[a] Categories are not exclusive.

[b] Includes only owners who have harvested.

[c] A commercial harvest is defined as the harvesting of saw logs, veneer logs, or pulpwood.

A limited number of family forest landowners formally develop a management plan or seek advice in managing their land for timber production or other forest-related amenities. Only 5 percent of the 163,000 private family forest landowners have a written management plan to help guide their land use decisions. Although few have a written plan, some 36,000 family forest landowners (22 percent) at least sought advice about managing their land. It is important to note that these numbers may be highly deflated because the total number of landowners is used to calculate the percentages and not all landowners in Mississippi are interested in forest land management, including maintaining written management plans. In addition, the size of many landholdings (< 10 acres, 25 percent of landholdings in the State) often precludes the ability of a landowner to actively manage for products such as timber, an activity that generally benefits from management plans and forestry professionals.

Table 12—Area and number of family-owned forests in Mississippi by recent (past 5 years) forestry activity, 2006

Activity[a]	Area		Owners	
	Acres	SE	Number	SE
	thousand	*percent*	*thousand*	*percent*
Timber harvest	5,885	8.5	30	20.1
Collection of NTFPs	1,022	31.0	3	57.1
Site preparation	4,548	10.3	19	26.7
Tree planting	5,873	8.1	28	20.5
Fire hazard reduction	3,636	12.0	25	42.5
Application of chemicals	3,496	12.6	17	34.3
Road/trail maintenance	4,603	10.1	5	34.3
Wildlife habitat improvement	3,814	11.4	8	35.5
Posting land	5,997	12.4	66	37.0
Private recreation	5,773	12.3	6	29.2
Public recreation	1,441	34.8	4	47.9
None of the above	2,279	17.3	75	26.4

SE = sampling error; NTFPs = nontimber forest products.
[a] Categories are not exclusive.

Wild turkey toms in autumn forest. (photo by Steve Maslowski, U.S. Fish and Wildlife Service)

Abt, K.L.; Winter, S.A.; Huggett, R.J., Jr. 2002. Local economic impacts of forests. In: Wear, D.N.; Greis, J.G., eds. Southern forest resource assessment. Gen. Tech. Rep. SRS–53. Asheville, NC: U.S. Department of Agriculture Forest Service, Southern Research Station: 239–267.

Bechtold, W.A.; Patterson, P.L., eds. 2005. The enhanced forest inventory and analysis program—national sampling design and estimation procedures. Gen. Tech. Rep. SRS–80. Asheville, NC: U.S. Department of Agriculture Forest Service, Southern Research Station. 85 p.

Beers, T.W.; Miller, C.I. 1964. Point sampling: research results, theory and applications. Resour. Bull. 786. Lafayette, IN: Purdue University Agricultural Experiment Station. 55 p. + insert.

Bentley, J.W.; Howell, M.; Johnson, T.G. 2008. Mississippi's timber industry—an assessment of timber product output and use, 2005. Resour. Bull. SRS–131. Asheville, NC: U.S. Department of Agriculture Forest Service, Southern Research Station. 32 p.

Bentley, J.W.; Johnson, T.G.; Howell, M. 2002. Mississippi's timber industry—an assessment of timber product output and use, 1999. Resour. Bull. SRS–80. Asheville, NC: U.S. Department of Agriculture Forest Service, Southern Research Station. 40 p.

Butler, B.J. 2008. Family forest owners of the United States, 2006. Gen. Tech. Rep. NRS–27. Newtown Square, PA: U.S. Department of Agriculture Forest Service, Northern Research Station. 72 p.

Chamberlain, J.L.; Predny, M. 2003. Non-timber forest products enterprises in the South: perceived distribution and implications for sustainable forest management. In: Miller, J.E.; Midtbo, J.M., eds. Proceedings, first national symposium on sustainable natural resource-based alternative enterprises. Mississippi State, MS: Mississippi State University Extension Service and Mississippi State University Forest and Wildlife Research Center: 48–63.

Clark, W.C., ed. 1982. Carbon dioxide review: 1982. New York: Oxford University Press. 469 p.

Cost, N.D. 1978. Multiresource inventories—a technique for measuring volumes in standing trees. Res. Pap. SE–196. Asheville, NC: U.S. Department of Agriculture Forest Service, Southeastern Forest Experiment Station. 18 p.

Eastern Forest Environmental Threat Assessment Center. 2007. Forest threat summary viewer. http://www.forestthreats.org/tools/forest-threat-summary-viewer. [Date accessed: December 21].

Graumann, A.; Houston, T.; Lawrimore, J. [and others]. 2005. Hurricane Katrina: a climatological perspective, preliminary report. Tech. Rep. 2005–01. Washington, DC: U.S. Department of Commerce, National Oceanic and Atmospheric Administration. 28 p.

Grosenbaugh, L.R. 1952. Plotless timber estimates—new, fast, easy. Journal of Forestry. 50(1): 32–37.

Homer, C.; Dewitz, J.; Fry, J. [and others]. 2007. Completion of the 2001 national land cover database for the conterminous United States. Photogrammetric Engineering and Remote Sensing. 73(4): 337–341.

Homer, C.; Huang, C.; Yang, L. [and others]. 2004. Development of a 2001 national land cover database for the United States. Photogrammetric Engineering and Remote Sensing. 70(7): 829–840.

Howell, M.; Johnson, T.G.; Bentley, J.W. 2005. Mississippi's timber industry—an assessment of timber product output and use, 2002. Resour. Bull. SRS–102. Asheville, NC: U.S. Department of Agriculture Forest Service, Southern Research Station. 45 p.

Johnsen, K.H.; Wear, D.N.; Oren, R. [and others]. 2001. Carbon sequestration and southern pine forests. Journal of Forestry. 99(4): 14–21.

Kellison, R.C.; Young, M.J. 1997. The bottomland hardwood forest of the Southern United States. Forest Ecology and Management. 90: 101–113.

King, S.L.; Keeland, B.D. 1999. Evaluation of reforestation in the lower Mississippi River Alluvial Valley. Restoration Ecology. 7(4): 348–359.

McNulty, S.G.; Aber, J.D. 2001. U.S. national climate change assessment on forest ecosystems: an introduction. BioScience. 51(9): 720–722.

Mississippi Forestry Commission. 2006. *Ips* engraver beetle. Tech. Bull. 1. http://www.mfc.state.ms.us/forest_health.htm. [Date accessed: October 16, 2008].

Mississippi State University, Cooperative Extension Service. 1995. 1995 harvest of forest products report. http://msucares.com/forestry/economics/reports/index.html. [Date accessed: November 5, 2007].

Mississippi State University, Cooperative Extension Service. 1996. 1996 harvest of forest products report. http://msucares.com/forestry/economics/reports/index.html. [Date accessed: November 5, 2007].

Mississippi State University, Cooperative Extension Service. 1997. 1997 harvest of forest products report. http://msucares.com/forestry/economics/reports/index.html. [Date accessed: November 5, 2007].

Mississippi State University, Cooperative Extension Service. 1998. 1998 harvest of forest products report. http://msucares.com/forestry/economics/reports/index.html. [Date accessed: November 5, 2007].

Mississippi State University, Cooperative Extension Service. 1999. 1999 harvest of forest products report. http://msucares.com/forestry/economics/reports/index.html. [Date accessed: November 5, 2007].

Mississippi State University, Cooperative Extension Service. 2000. 2000 harvest of forest products report. http://msucares.com/forestry/economics/reports/index.html. [Date accessed: November 5, 2007].

Mississippi State University, Cooperative Extension Service. 2001. 2001 harvest of forest products report. http://msucares.com/forestry/economics/reports/index.html. [Date accessed: November 5, 2007].

Mississippi State University, Cooperative Extension Service. 2002. 2002 harvest of forest products report. http://msucares.com/forestry/economics/reports/index.html. [Date accessed: November 5, 2007].

Mississippi State University, Cooperative Extension Service. 2003. 2003 harvest of forest products report. http://msucares.com/forestry/economics/reports/index.html. [Date accessed: November 5, 2007].

Mississippi State University, Cooperative Extension Service. 2004. 2004 harvest of forest products report. http://msucares.com/forestry/economics/reports/index.html. [Date accessed: November 5, 2007].

Mississippi State University, Cooperative Extension Service. 2005. 2005 harvest of forest products report. http://msucares.com/forestry/economics/reports/index.html. [Date accessed: November 5, 2007].

Mississippi State University, Cooperative Extension Service. 2006. 2006 harvest of forest products report. http://msucares.com/forestry/economics/reports/index.html. [Date accessed: November 5, 2007].

Montreal Process Working Group. 2005. The Montreal process. http://www.rinya.maff.go.jp/mpci/. [Date accessed: January 14, 2008].

Nabuurs, G.-J.; Ravindranath, N.H.; Paustian, K. [and others]. 2004. LUCF-sector good practice guidance. In: Penman, J.; Gytarsky, M.; Hirishi, T. [and others], eds. Intergovernmental panel on climate change, good practice guidance for land use, land-use change and forestry. Hayama, Japan: Institute for Global Environmental Strategies:

National Oceanic and Atmospheric Administration. 2007. National environmental satellite data and information service. http://www4.ncdc.noaa.gov/cgi-win/wwcgi.dll?wwevent~storms. [Date accessed: December 2].

Oswalt, C.M.; Oswalt, S.N.; Clatterbuck, W.K. 2007. Effects of *Microstegium vimineum* (Trin.) A. Camus on native woody species density and diversity in a productive mixed-hardwood forest in Tennessee. Forest Ecology and Management. 242: 727–732.

Oswalt, C.M.; Oswalt, S.N.; Johnson, T.G. [and others]. 2009. Tennessee's forests, 2004. Resour. Bull. SRS–144. Asheville, NC: U.S. Department of Agriculture Forest Service, Southern Research Station. 96 p.

Pye, J.M.; Price, T.S.; Clarke, S.R.; Huggett, R.J., Jr. 2004. A history of southern pine beetle outbreaks in the Southeastern United States through 2004. www.srs.fs.usda.gov/econ/data/spb/outbrk.htm. [Date accessed: April 9, 2008].

Reams, G.A.; Smith, W.D.; Hansen, M.H. [and others]. 2005. The forest inventory and analysis sampling frame. In: Bechtold, W.A.; Patterson, P.L., eds. The enhanced forest inventory and analysis program—national sampling design and estimation procedures. Gen. Tech. Rep. SRS–80. Asheville, NC: U.S. Department of Agriculture Forest Service, Southern Research Station: 11–26.

Riitters, K.H.; Wickham, J.D.; O'Neill, R.V. [and others]. 2002. Fragmentation of continental United States forests. Ecosystems. 5: 815–822.

Rosson, J.F., Jr. 2001. Forest resources of Mississippi, 1994. Resour. Bull. SRS–61. Asheville, NC: U.S. Department of Agriculture Forest Service, Southern Research Station. 78 p.

Spetich, M.A.; Parker, G.R. 1998. Distribution of biomass in an Indiana old-growth forest from 1926-1992. American Midland Naturalist. 139: 90–107.

Stratton, D.P.; Howell, M.; Romedy, R. 1998. Mississippi's timber industry—an assessment of timber product output and use, 1995. Resour. Bull. SRS–29. Asheville, NC: U.S. Department of Agriculture Forest Service, Southern Research Station. 23 p.

U.S. Department of Agriculture Forest Service. 2004. National report on sustainable forests—2003. FS–766. Washington, DC. 139 p.

U.S. Department of Agriculture Forest Service. 2005. Forest inventory and analysis national core field guide. Field data collection for phase 2 plots. Version 3.0. Arlington, VA: U.S. Department of Agriculture Forest Service, Forest Inventory and Analysis Program. Vol. 1. http://fia.fs.fed.us/library/field-guides-methods-proc/docs/2006/core_ver_3-0_10_2005.pdf. [Date accessed: July 7, 2008].

U.S. Department of Commerce, Bureau of the Census. 2005. Statistics for the United States and States by industry group; 2005 and earlier years. Washington, DC: U.S. Government Printing Office.

Van Deusen, P.C.; Dell, T.R.; Thomas, C.E. 1986. Volume growth estimation from permanent horizontal points. Forest Science. 32(2): 415–422.

Below is a list of commonly used technical terms and their definitions. For additional details, including measurement protocols, see the Southern Research Station's field manual Web site (U.S. Department of Agriculture Forest Service 2005). A discussion of changes to standard terminology since earlier surveys is included in the section on inventory methods.

Afforestation. Area of land previously classified as nonforest that is converted to forest by planting of trees or by natural reversion to forest.

Average annual mortality. Average annual volume of trees ≥ 5.0 inches d.b.h. that died from natural causes during the intersurvey period.

Average annual removals. Average annual volume of trees ≥ 5.0 inches d.b.h. removed from the inventory by harvesting, cultural operations (such as timber-stand improvement), land clearing, or changes in land use during the intersurvey period.

Average net annual growth. Average annual net change in volume of trees ≥ 5.0 inches d.b.h. in the absence of cutting (gross growth minus mortality) during the intersurvey period.

Basal area. The area in square feet of the cross section at breast height of a single tree or of all the trees in a stand, usually expressed in square feet per acre.

Biomass. The aboveground fresh weight of solid wood and bark in live trees ≥ 1.0 inch d.b.h. from the ground to the tip of the tree. All foliage is excluded. The weight of wood and bark in lateral limbs, secondary limbs, and twigs under 0.5 inch in diameter at the point of occurrence on sapling-size trees is included but is excluded on poletimber and sawtimber-size trees.

Blind check. A remeasurement done by a qualified inspection crew without production crew data on hand; a full remeasurement of the plot is recommended for the purpose of obtaining a measure of data quality. If a full plot remeasurement is not possible, then it is strongly recommended that at least two full subplots be completely remeasured along with all the plot level information. The two datasets are maintained separately. Discrepancies between the two sets of data are not reconciled. Blind checks are done on production plots only. This procedure provides a quality assessment and evaluation function. The statistics band recommends a random subset of plots be chosen for remeasurement.

Bole. That portion of a tree between a 1-foot stump and a 4-inch top d.o.b. in trees ≥ 5.0 inches d.b.h.

Census water. Streams, sloughs, estuaries, canals, and other moving bodies of water ≥ 200 feet wide, and lakes, reservoirs, ponds, and other permanent bodies of water ≥ 4.5 acres in area.

Cold check. An inspection done either as part of the training process, or as part of the ongoing QC program. Normally the installation crew is not present at the time of inspection. The inspector has the completed data in hand at the time of inspection. The inspection can include the whole plot or a subset of the plot. Data errors are corrected. Cold checks are done on production plots only. This type of QC measurement is a "blind" measurement in that the crews do not know when or which of their plots will be remeasured by the inspection crew and cannot, therefore, alter their performance because of knowledge that the plot is a QA plot.

Compacted area. Type of compaction measured as part of the soil indicator. Examples include the junction areas of skid trails, landing areas, work areas, etc.

Condition class. The combination of discrete landscape and forest attributes that identify, define, and stratify the area associated with a plot. Examples of such attributes include condition status, forest type, stand origin, stand size, owner group, reserve status, and stand density.

Crown. The part of a tree or woody plant bearing live branches or foliage.

D.b.h. Tree diameter in inches (outside bark) at breast height (4.5 feet aboveground).

Diameter class. A classification of trees based on tree d.b.h. Two-inch diameter classes are commonly used by Forest Inventory and Analysis, with the even inch as the approximate midpoint for a class. For example, the 6-inch class includes trees 5.0 through 6.9 inches d.b.h.

Erosion. The wearing away of the land surface by running water, wind, ice, or other geological agents.

Forest land. Land at least 10 percent stocked by forest trees of any size, or formerly having had such tree cover, and not currently developed for nonforest use. The minimum area considered for classification is 1 acre. Forested strips must be at least 120 feet wide.

Forest management type. A classification of timberland based on forest type and stand origin.

Pine plantation. Stands that (1) have been artificially regenerated by planting or direct seeding, (2) are classed as a pine or other softwood forest type, and (3) have at least 10 percent stocking.

Natural pine. Stands that (1) have not been artificially regenerated, (2) are classed as a pine or other softwood forest type, and (3) have at least 10 percent stocking.

Oak-pine. Stands that have at least 10 percent stocking and classed as a forest type of oak-pine.

Upland hardwood. Stands that have at least 10 percent stocking and classed as an oak-hickory or maple-beech-birch forest type.

Lowland or bottomland hardwood. Stands that have at least 10 percent stocking with a forest type of oak-gum-cypress, elm-ash-cottonwood, palm, or other tropical.

Nonstocked stands. Stands < 10 percent stocked with live trees.

Forest type. A classification of forest land based on the species forming a plurality of live-tree stocking. Major eastern forest-type groups are:

White-red-jack pine. Forests in which eastern white pine, red pine, or jack pine, singly or in combination, constitute a plurality of the stocking. (Common associates include hemlock, birch, and maple.)

Spruce-fir. Forests in which spruce or true firs, singly or in combination, constitute a plurality of the stocking. (Common associates include maple, birch, and hemlock.)

Longleaf-slash pine. Forests in which longleaf or slash pine, singly or in combination, constitute a plurality of the stocking. (Common associates include oak, hickory, and gum.)

Loblolly-shortleaf pine. Forests in which loblolly pine, shortleaf pine, or other southern yellow pines, except longleaf or slash pine, singly or in combination, constitute a plurality of the stocking. (Common associates include oak, hickory, and gum.)

Oak-pine. Forests in which hardwoods (usually upland oaks) constitute a plurality of the stocking but in which pines account for 25 to 50 percent of the stocking. (Common associates include gum, hickory, and yellow-poplar.)

Oak-hickory. Forests in which upland oaks or hickory, singly or in combination, constitute a plurality of the stocking, except where pines account for 25 to 50 percent, in which case the stand would be classified oak-pine. (Common associates include yellow-poplar, elm, maple, and black walnut.)

Oak-gum-cypress. Bottomland forests in which tupelo, blackgum, sweetgum, oaks, or southern cypress, singly or in combination, constitute a plurality of the stocking, except where pines account for 25 to 50 percent of stocking, in which case the stand would be classified as oak-pine. (Common associates include cottonwood, willow, ash, elm, hackberry, and maple.)

Elm-ash-cottonwood. Forests in which elm, ash, or cottonwood, singly or in combination, constitute a plurality of the stocking. (Common associates include willow, sycamore, beech, and maple.)

Maple-beech-birch. Forests in which maple, beech, or yellow birch, singly or in combination, constitute a plurality of the stocking. (Common associates include hemlock, elm, basswood, and white pine.)

Nonstocked stands. Stands < 10 percent stocked with live trees.

Forested tract size. The area of forest within the contiguous tract containing each Forest Inventory and Analysis sample plot.

Fresh weight. Mass of tree component at time of cutting.

Gross growth. Annual increase in volume of trees ≥ 5.0 inches d.b.h. in the absence of cutting and mortality. (Gross growth includes survivor growth, ingrowth, growth on ingrowth, growth on removals before removal, and growth on mortality before death.)

Growing-stock trees. Living trees of commercial species classified as sawtimber, poletimber, saplings, and seedlings. Trees must contain at least one 12-foot or two 8-foot logs in the saw-log portion, currently or potentially (if too small to qualify), to be classed as growing stock. The log(s) must meet dimension and merchantability standards to qualify. Trees must also have, currently or potentially, one-third of the gross board-foot volume in sound wood.

Growing-stock volume. The cubic-foot volume of sound wood in growing-stock trees at least 5.0 inches d.b.h. from a 1-foot stump to a minimum 4.0-inch top d.o.b. of the central stem.

Hardwoods. Dicotyledonous trees, usually broadleaf and deciduous.

Soft hardwoods. Hardwood species with an average specific gravity of ≤ 0.50, such as gums, yellow-poplar, cottonwoods, red maple, basswoods, and willows.

Hard hardwoods. Hardwood species with an average specific gravity > 0.50 such as oaks, hard maples, hickories, and beech.

Hexagonal grid (hex). A hexagonal grid formed from equilateral triangles for the purpose of tessellating the Forest Inventory and Analysis inventory sample. Each hexagon in the base grid has an area of 5,937 acres (2403.6 ha) and contains one inventory plot. The base grid can be subdivided into smaller hexagons to intensify the sample.

Land area. The area of dry land and land temporarily or partly covered by water, such as marshes, swamps, and river floodplains (omitting tidal flats below mean high tide), streams, sloughs, estuaries, and canals < 200 feet wide, and lakes, reservoirs, and ponds < 4.5 acres in area.

Live trees. All living trees. All size classes, all tree classes, and both commercial and noncommercial species are included.

Measurement quality objective (MQO). A data user's estimate of the precision, bias, and completeness of data necessary to satisfy a prescribed application, e.g., Resource Planning Act, assessments by State foresters, forest planning, forest health analyses. Describes the acceptable tolerance for each data element. MQOs consist of two parts: a statement of the tolerance and a percentage of time when the collected data are required to be within tolerance. MQOs can only be assigned where standard methods of sampling or field measurements exist, or where experience has established upper or lower bounds on precision or bias. MQOs can be set for measured data elements, observed data elements, and derived data elements.

Net annual change. Increase or decrease in volume of live trees at least 5.0 inches d.b.h. Net annual change is equal to net annual growth minus average annual removals.

Noncommercial species. Tree species of typically small size, poor form, or inferior quality that normally do not develop into trees suitable for industrial wood products.

Nonforest land. Land that has never supported forests and land formerly forested where timber production is precluded by development for other uses.

Nonstocked stands. Stands < 10 percent stocked with live trees.

Other forest land. Forest land other than timberland and productive-reserved forest land. It includes available and reserved forest land which is incapable of producing annually 20 cubic feet per acre of industrial wood under natural conditions, because of adverse site conditions such as sterile soils, dry climate, poor drainage, high elevation, steepness, or rockiness.

Other removals. The growing-stock volume of trees removed from the inventory by cultural operations such as timber stand improvement, land clearing, and other changes in land use, resulting in the removal of the trees from timberland.

Ownership. The property owned by one ownership unit, including all parcels of land in the United States.

National forest land. Federal land that has been legally designated as national forests or purchase units, and other land under the administration of the Forest Service, including experimental areas and Bankhead-Jones Title III land.

Forest industry land. Land owned by companies or individuals operating primary wood-using plants.

Nonindustrial private forest land. Privately owned land excluding forest industry land.

Corporate. Owned by corporations, including incorporated farm ownerships.

Individual. All lands owned by individuals, including farm operators.

Other public. An ownership class that includes all public lands except national forests.

Miscellaneous Federal land. Federal land other than national forests.

State, county, and municipal land. Land owned by States, counties, and local public agencies or municipalities or land leased to these governmental units for ≥ 50 years.

Phase 1 (P1). Forest Inventory and Analysis activities related to remote-sensing, the primary purpose of which is to label plots and obtain stratum weights for population estimates.

Phase 2 (P2). Forest Inventory and Analysis activities conducted on the network of ground plots. The primary purpose is to obtain field data that enable classification and summarization of area, tree, and other attributes associated with forest land uses.

Phase 3 (P3). Forest Inventory and Analysis activities conducted on a subset of phase 2 plots. Additional attributes related to forest health are measured on phase 3 plots.

Poletimber-size trees. Softwoods 5.0 to 8.9 inches d.b.h. and hardwoods 5.0 to 10.9 inches d.b.h.

Productive-reserved forest land. Forest land sufficiently productive to qualify as timberland but withdrawn from timber utilization through statute or administrative regulation.

Quality assurance (QA). The total integrated program for ensuring that the uncertainties inherent in Forest Inventory and Analysis data are known and do not exceed acceptable magnitudes, within a stated level of confidence. QA encompasses the plans, specifications, and policies affecting the collection, processing, and reporting of data. It is the system of activities designed to provide program managers and project leaders with independent assurance that total system quality control is being effectively implemented.

Quality control (QC). The routine application of prescribed field and laboratory procedures, e.g., random check cruising, periodic calibration, instrument maintenance, use of certified standards, etc., in order to reduce random and systematic errors and ensure that data are generated within known and acceptable performance limits. QC also ensures the use of qualified personnel, reliable equipment and supplies, training of personnel, good field and laboratory practices, and strict adherence to standard operating procedures.

Reforestation. Area of land previously classified as forest that is regenerated by tree planting or natural regeneration.

Rotten trees. Live trees of commercial species not containing at least one 12-foot saw log, or two noncontiguous saw logs, each 8 feet or longer, now or prospectively, primarily because of rot or missing sections, and with less than one-third of the gross board-foot tree volume in sound material.

Rough trees. Live trees of commercial species not containing at least one 12-foot saw log, or two noncontiguous saw logs, each 8 feet or longer, now or prospectively, primarily because of roughness, poor form, splits, and cracks, and with less than one-third of the gross board-foot tree volume in sound material; and live trees of noncommercial species.

Sapling. Live trees 1.0 to 4.9 inches (2.5 to 12.5 cm) in diameter (d.b.h.).

Saw log. A log meeting minimum standards of diameter, length, and defect, including logs at least 8 feet long, sound and straight, with a minimum diameter inside bark for softwoods of 6 inches (8 inches for hardwoods).

Saw-log portion. The part of the bole of sawtimber trees between a 1-foot stump and the saw-log top.

Saw-log top. The point on the bole of sawtimber trees above which a conventional saw log cannot be produced. The minimum saw-log top is 7.0 inches d.o.b. for softwoods and 9.0 inches d.o.b. for hardwoods.

Sawtimber-size trees. Softwoods ≥ 9.0 inches d.b.h. and hardwoods ≥ 11.0 inches d.b.h.

Sawtimber volume. Growing-stock volume in the saw-log portion of sawtimber-size trees in board feet (International 1/4-inch rule).

Seedlings. Trees < 1.0 inch d.b.h. and > 1 foot tall for hardwoods, > 6 inches tall for softwoods, and > 0.5 inch in diameter at ground level for longleaf pine.

Select red oaks. A group of several red oak species composed of cherrybark, Shumard, and northern red oaks. Other red oak species are included in the "other red oaks" group.

Select white oaks. A group of several white oak species composed of white, swamp chestnut, swamp white, chinkapin, Durand, and bur oaks. Other white oak species are included in the "other white oaks" group.

Site class. A classification of forest land in terms of potential capacity to grow crops of industrial wood based on fully stocked natural stands.

Softwoods. Coniferous trees, usually evergreen, having leaves that are needles or scalelike.

Yellow pines. Loblolly, longleaf, slash, pond, shortleaf, pitch, Virginia, sand, spruce, and Table Mountain pines.

Other softwoods. Cypress, eastern redcedar, white-cedar, eastern white pine, eastern hemlock, spruce, and fir.

Stand age. The average age of dominant and codominant trees in the stand.

Stand origin. A classification of forest stands describing their means of origin.

Planted. Planted or artificially seeded.

Natural. No evidence of artificial regeneration.

Stand-size class. A classification of forest land based on the diameter class distribution of live trees in the stand.

Sawtimber stands. Stands at least 10 percent stocked with live trees, with one-half or more of total stocking in sawtimber and poletimber trees, and with sawtimber stocking at least equal to poletimber stocking.

Poletimber stands. Stands at least 10 percent stocked with live trees, with one-half or more of total stocking in poletimber and sawtimber trees, and with poletimber stocking exceeding sawtimber stocking.

Sapling-seedling stands. Stands at least 10 percent stocked with live trees, in which saplings and seedlings account for more than one-half of total stocking.

Nonstocked stands. Stands < 10 percent stocked with live trees.

Stocking. The degree of occupancy of land by trees, measured by basal area or the number of trees in a stand and spacing in the stand, compared with a minimum standard, depending on tree size, required to fully utilize the growth potential of the land.

Density of trees and basal area per acre required for full stocking:

D.b.h. class	Trees per acre for full stocking	Basal area
inches		square feet per acre
Seedlings	600	—
2	560	—
4	460	—
6	340	67
8	240	84
10	155	85
12	115	90
14	90	96
16	72	101
18	60	106
20	51	111

— = not applicable.

Timberland. Forest land capable of producing 20 cubic feet of industrial wood per acre per year and not withdrawn from timber utilization.

Tree. Woody plant having one erect perennial stem or trunk at least 3 inches d.b.h., a more or less definitely formed crown of foliage, and a height of at least 13 feet (at maturity).

Tree grade. A classification of the saw-log portion of sawtimber trees based on: (1) the grade of the butt log or (2) the ability to produce at least one 12-foot or two 8-foot logs in the upper section of the saw-log portion. Tree grade is an indicator of quality; grade 1 is the best quality.

Upper-stem portion. The part of the main stem or fork of sawtimber trees above the saw-log top to a minimum top diameter of 4.0 inches outside bark or to the point where the main stem or fork breaks into limbs.

Volume of live trees. The cubic-foot volume of sound wood in live trees at least 5.0 inches d.b.h. from a 1-foot stump to a minimum 4.0-inch top d.o.b. of the central stem.

Volume of saw-log portion of sawtimber trees. The cubic-foot volume of sound wood in the saw-log portion of sawtimber trees. Volume is the net result after deductions for rot, sweep, and other defects that affect use for lumber.

Metric equivalents

1 acre = 4046.86 m^2 or 0.405 ha
1,000 acres = 404.7 ha
1,000 cubic feet = 28.3 m^3
1 cubic foot per acre = 0.07 m^3/ha
1 foot = 0.3048 m
1 inch = 2.54 cm
1 mile = 1.609 km

Common yellowthroat. (photo by Dave Menke, U.S. Fish and Wildlife Service)

University of Tennessee, Knoxville, Extension Professor Wayne Clatterbuck collects research data on trees planted at Noxubee Wildlife Refuge in Mississippi. (photo by Christoper M. Oswalt)

A State-by-State inventory of the Nation's forest land began in the mid-1930s. These surveys primarily were designed and conducted to provide estimates of forest area; wood volume; and growth, removals, and mortality. Throughout the years, national concerns over perceived and real trends in forest resource conditions, and numerous technical innovations have led to an array of improvements (Reams and others 2005). The primary purpose for conducting forest inventories has remained unchanged, but the methods have undergone substantial change. The following is a general description of the sample design currently used to collect the information and of the procedures used to derive the forest resource estimates provided in this report. A brief discussion of past sample designs and procedures are included to alert users to substantive changes. These changes necessitate caution in making comparisons with previous forest resource estimates.

Sample Design

Current annual fixed-area inventory system—Beginning in 1995, the FIA Program began efforts to standardize an inventory design to be used in all States. The current FIA inventory is a three-phase, fixed-plot sample survey conducted on an annual basis. Phase 1 (P1) procedures produce estimates of forest and nonforest area based on national land cover data.

Phase 2 (P2) procedures involve field visits to ground sample locations and establishment or remeasurement of a series of samples containing forest land. At forest land locations, field crews take tree measurements and collect other information to derive estimates of forest area, wood volume, tree growth, removals and mortality, and other attributes. P2 observations occur annually on a portion of the total sample locations in each State. A year's worth of data collection is called

Forest Inventory and Analysis foresters on a plot in Mississippi.
(photo by Andrew Edwards, U.S. Forest Service)

a panel. A complete measurement cycle is composed of typically between five and seven panels of data. Annual observations provide the means to update forest resource information each year, although complete cycle time may differ slightly by State. The estimates in this Mississippi report are based on a full five-panel cycle conducted from 2005 to 2007, clearly less than the normal 5 years for a cycle. Subsequent measurements will be on a one-annual-panel-per-year schedule.

Phase 3 (P3) procedures involve sampling on a subset (1/16th) of the P2 sample locations. P3 measurements are combined with P2 measurements to assess the overall health of forested ecosystems within each State.

Previous periodic, variable-, and fixed-radius inventory system—Previously, the FIA Program typically conducted surveys one State at a time. Each State was collected within a period of 1 to 2 years, not unlike this survey of Mississippi. This "periodic" inventory system was designed to provide updated forest resource estimates for all States every 7 to 10 years. Unlike the current survey of Mississippi, field crews collecting periodic data used a 10-point prism sampling (variable-radius) technique (Grosenbaugh 1952) for large trees and fixed-radius subplots on the first 3 points for smaller trees. The layout of the cluster of points varied in some cases to force the 2nd through 10th points into a forest condition. The following section offers a more detailed discussion of the changes in plot design and layout of the plot cluster.

Changes in Plot Design

Current plot design—The current annual survey employs a fixed-plot cluster composed of four 24-foot radius (1/24 of an acre) subplots with centers spaced 120 feet apart (Bechtold and Patterson 2005). The cumulative sample area of these four subplots is one-sixth of an acre. The cluster plot is a 1.5-acre circle that circumscribes the outer boundary of the three outer subplots. Trees ≥ 5 inches d.b.h. are measured on each subplot. Trees ≥ 1.0 but < 5.0 inches d.b.h. and seedlings (< 1.0 inch d.b.h.) are measured on a microplot (1/300 of an acre; 6.8-foot radius) on each of the four subplots. The microplot is offset 12 feet at 90 degrees from the subplot center.

A unique feature of this plot design is in the mapping of different land use and forest conditions that are encountered on the cluster plot. Since the plots are placed on the ground without bias, i.e., systematically but at a scale large enough to be considered random, there is a probability that the cluster plot will straddle more than one type of land use or forest condition. When this does occur, a boundary is drawn across the plot so that the different homogeneous units are identified and isolated.

There are two steps in the mapping process. The first step involves identifying forest and nonforest areas on the plot and establishing a boundary line on the plot if both are present. The second step involves identifying homogeneous areas in the forested portion of the plot based on six factors: (1) forest type, (2) stand size, (3) ownership, (4) stand density, (5) regeneration status, and (6) reserved status. These, too, are mapped into separate entities.

Previous plot design—In the 1994 Mississippi inventory, FIA utilized a prism sampling technique for large trees and fixed-radius subplots for smaller trees. At each forested location, field crews installed a cluster plot consisting of 10 equally spaced satellite points 66 feet apart, distributed

over an area about 1 acre in size. At each forested sample plot, crews selected trees ≥ 5.0 inches d.b.h. with a 37.5 basal-area-factor (BAF) prism at each of the satellite points. Therefore, each tree selected with the prism across the 10 points represented 3.75 square feet of basal area. Trees < 5.0 but ≥ 1.0 inch d.b.h. and seedlings (< 1.0 inch d.b.h.) were tallied on a 7.1-foot radius (1/275-acre circle) fixed plot that was located at the center of the first three satellite points (Rosson 2001).

There was no mapping of the forest condition or forest-nonforest boundary, or estimation of pattern metrics. Field crews used plot center (point 1) to identify the land use for the entire cluster plot as either forest or nonforest. In situations where field crews encountered a forested plot center and the cluster plot straddled a forest-nonforest boundary, crews rotated any points that fell in the nonforest portion into the forest condition according to a predefined protocol, so that each point was at least 66 feet apart from another point. In addition, crews rotated points into a forest condition if the points were located within 33 feet of a nonforest boundary. If all 10 points were on forest land and straddled more than one forest condition, crews in Mississippi did not rotate points into homogeneous forest conditions.

Determining Forest Resource Statistics

The changes in sample design and plot layout changed the derivation of basic resource statistics, e.g., forest area, stocking, growth, removals, and mortality. The following section briefly describes the methods and processes used and explains how they have changed with the transition from the previous to the current inventory system.

Estimating Forest Area

Annual inventory system—FIA bases the three phases of the current sampling method on a hexagonal grid (hex) design, with each successive phase sampled with less intensity. There are 16 P2 hexes for every P3 hex, and 27 P1 hexes for every P2 hex. P1 hexes represent about 222 acres, while P2 and P3 hexes represent roughly 6,000 and 96,000 acres, respectively.

P1 involves assigning a plot to the P1 hexes on digital imagery—currently FIA uses the National Land Cover Database (NLCD). Each hex point, or "dot," is classified as either forest or nonforest and a percentage for each class is derived for the entire State. The P1 point classifications are then checked at permanent ground sample locations that make up the P2 sample. Two correction factors are created by comparing the forest and nonforest classifications on the digital imagery to the classifications of the same points made at ground sample locations. These correction factors are used to adjust the percent forest derived from the original (P1) estimate. The correction factors also adjust for possible misclassifications in the NLCD and for change on the ground that occurred since the date of the digital imagery used for land cover classification.

P2 locations generally are not placed in the center of the hex. If a sample location from a prior inventory exists in a P2 hex, then that same location is used again. If two sample locations from a prior survey existed with the same hex, then one is dropped. For P2 hexes containing no prior sample location, a new sample location is created at a random point within the hex. This process is performed in a manner that maintains as many existing plots as possible.

Periodic inventory system—Ground sample locations were placed at the intersection of lines on a 3-mile grid lain over each State. Theoretically, each plot represented 5,760 acres of forest land. Area estimation was based on photointerpreting the ground use of each plot and 25 photo sample points around each plot. The ratio of forest-to-nonforest dots provided the percent forest for each county. Field crew personnel determined the actual ground use of the plot at the time it was sampled. Percent forest for each county was calculated using the same methods and procedures used for the current survey.

During the 1970s, the sampling intensity was increased by adding a 6-mile grid within the 3-mile grid. The plot centers and 25 associated sample points of these plots were photointerpreted and verified by the field crews. No additional information was gathered from these locations. These plots were referred to as "supplemental" plots and their sole purpose was to strengthen the area estimation sample.

Estimating stocking, forest type, and stand-product class—FIA now uses new procedures for associating forest type and stand-product classes with each condition observed on a plot. The procedures, definitions, and associated algorithms are designed by FIA nationally to provide consistency among States. The list of recognized forest types, groupings of these forest types for reporting purposes, models used to assign stocking values to individual trees, and names given to the forest types have changed.

Stocking (the density value assigned to a sampled live tree expressed as a percentage of the total tree density required to fully utilize the growth potential of the land) is the basis for calculating stand size and forest type. Procedures used to assign stocking to individual trees differ with the change in survey design. Following is a brief summary of recent past and current methods used to calculate stocking and to estimate forest type and stand size.

Current fixed-radius tree tally—Currently, stand-product and forest-type classifications are based on a computation of stocking from tallied trees by forest condition. Samples are of forest conditions that fall within four 24-foot-radius circular plots that are equally distributed within an area about 1.5 acres in size. Observations recorded include a seedling (< 1.0 inch d.b.h.) count and a tally of all live trees 1.0 to 4.9 inches d.b.h. on a 6.8-foot-radius microplot, and a tally of all live trees ≥ 5.0 inches d.b.h. for each 24-foot-radius plot.

Previous variable and fixed-radius tree tally—FIA surveys conducted from the 1970s to the 1990s based forest type and stand-product (a.k.a., stand size) classifications on a computation of stocking for tallied trees from a maximum of 10 sample points per forest land location. Trees 1.0 to 4.9 inches d.b.h. were tallied on a 6.8-foot-radius microplot. Trees ≥ 5.0 inches d.b.h. were selected with a 37.5-BAF prism sample (proportional to size). Seedlings (< 1.0 inch d.b.h.) were tallied only if no larger trees were present.

Forest type—Forest type is based upon and named for the tree species that forms the plurality of live-tree stocking if at least 10 percent stocked with live trees. The forest type indicates the predominant live-tree species cover. Hardwoods and softwoods are first aggregated to determine the predominant group, and forest type is selected from the predominant group. Eastern softwood groups have ≥ 50 percent softwood stocking and contain the named species that constitute a plurality of the stocking; the oak-pine group and hardwood groups have < 50 percent softwood stocking. The nonstocked group includes stands < 10 percent stocked with live trees.

Under the variable-radius sample design, a single forest type was determined for the entire plot regardless of the number of forest conditions present. The current fixed-radius inventory design identifies a forest type for each forest condition.

Stand-product (size) class—Stand-product class is a computed classification of forest land based on the diameter class distribution of live trees in the stand. Under the variable-radius sample design, a single stand-product class was derived for the entire plot regardless of the number of forest conditions present. Under the current, fixed-radius inventory design, a stand-product class is identified for each condition. Stand-product class is synonymous with stand-size class as the latter term is used in the forestry literature.

Estimating volume—Currently, FIA computes tree volume using a simple linear regression model (D^2H) that predicts gross cubic-foot volume inside bark from a 1-foot stump to a 4-inch upper diameter outside bark for each sample tree based on d.b.h. (D) and total height (H). Separate equation coefficients for 77 species or species groupings, developed from standing and felled-tree volume studies conducted across several Southern States, are used. Volume in forks or limbs outside of the main bole is excluded. FIA derives net cubic-foot volume by subtracting a field crew estimate of rotten or missing wood for each sample tree. Volume of the saw-log portion (expressed in International 1/4-inch board feet and in cubic feet) of sample trees is computed using board foot-cubic foot ratio equations.

Methods used to estimate tree volumes in the previous inventory differed from those described above. FIA derived tree volume from several measurements on each tree tallied on forested sample plots. These measurements included d.b.h., bark thickness, total height, bole length, log length, and up to four upper-stem diameters that defined pole top, pole mid, saw top, and saw mid. Gross tree volumes (cubic- and board-foot values) were determined by applying the formula for a conic frustum to sections of the bole. The volumes of the sections were then added together to produce a total stem volume. Obtaining net cubic-foot volume involved subtracting

a field crew estimate of rotten or missing wood for each sample tree. Merchantable volume was calculated from measurements of the bole from a 1-foot stump to an upper-stem stopping point determined by merchantability standards. The upper-stem diameter at this point could be as low as 4 inches but often was larger depending upon the perceived condition and product merchantability of the upper tree bole.

Because of these differences in volume computation and merchantability standards, previously reported volumes are not comparable to those reported in the current inventory. Previous tree volumes were recomputed using current equations for comparison. On average, the recomputed values for the 1994 tallied trees were higher than the original volumes for both softwood and hardwood species. The revisions are greater for hardwood species than softwoods and greater for trees with large d.b.h. compared with small d.b.h.

Estimating growth, removals, and mortality—One of the primary reasons for conducting forest inventories is to determine how much wood volume currently resides in southern forest stands, and to identify how and why it is changing. Estimates of growth, removals, and mortality provide some of the information needed to understand the change in volume. The following is a discussion of the current and past methods used.

Volume change components were derived from data collected during the remeasurement of sample plots established in the previous inventory. The plot design for the previous inventory was based on a cluster of 10 prism points established at intervals of 66 feet. The center of prism point 1 and the center of subplot 1 in the new plot design are the same point. Previously, at each prism point, trees ≥ 5.0 inches d.b.h. were selected with a 37.5-BAF prism. Trees < 5.0 inches d.b.h. but ≥ 1.0 inch d.b.h. were tallied on three

1/275-acre circular fixed plots, each of which was centered at one of the first three prism points.

At the time of remeasurement, some changes were made to the previous sample design. For trees <5.0 inches d.b.h. but ≥1.0 inch d.b.h., the 1/275-acre circular fixed plots at prism points 1, 2, and 3 were reduced to 1/300-acre circular fixed plots. For trees that were ≥5.0 inches d.b.h., only the first 5 of the 10 prism points were sampled at remeasurement. This means that prism points 1 through 5 carry twice the weight as in the previous inventory.

The former southern FIA unit estimated growth components using a Beers and Miller (1964) approach, as modified by Van Deusen and others (1986). The Van Deusen modification included new trees that grew into the prism sample. However, for this remeasurement, crews measured only survivor trees for growth. The only new tally trees on the prism points were those trees missed by the previous crew or those that were determined to be "through growth" (trees that previously were <1.0 inch d.b.h. on the 1/300-acre fixed circular plot at prism points 1 to 3 and that grew to ≥5.0 inches d.b.h. since the previous survey). Additionally, on reversions (previously nonforest land that has since reverted to forest land), all trees ≥5.0 inches d.b.h. in the new subplot design located in the reverted forested condition were evaluated to determine if they qualified as remeasured 37.5-BAF tally trees (based on d.b.h. and distance).

For Mississippi, users wishing to make rigorous comparisons of data between surveys should be aware of the substantive differences between the 2006 and 1994 plot designs. The most valuable trend information comes from plots revisited from one survey to the next and measured in the same way.

Although the 2006 and earlier plot designs may be judged statistically valid, the naturally occurring noise in the data hinders confident and rigorous trend assessments over time. When a design changes or plots are not remeasured, the true impact of such a change on trend analysis is unknown. The only way to quantify this impact with certainty would be to make measurements using both plot designs simultaneously and compare the results of these two independent surveys. Neither time nor money was available to do this. Below is a summary of changes:

Growth estimation—The 1994 inventory used the Van Deusen modification. For the 2006 survey, the Beers and Miller procedure was used. The two procedures differ in whether "ongrowth" trees on the prism plots are part of the growth components and in how trees per acre is calculated. Both methods are known to be unbiased, but the inclusion of "ongrowth" trees can affect how growth is distributed among product classes that are defined in terms of tree size.

Volume estimation—As documented earlier, in the estimating volume section, there were notable differences in how volumes were calculated in the two inventories. These differences also affect growth, removal, and mortality comparisons between 1994 and 2006. It was not possible to recompute the 1994 change components in the same way that inventory estimates were recomputed. Thus, the reader should use some discretion in evaluating trends in net growth, removals, and mortality between 1994 and 2006. This cautionary statement especially applies to hardwoods and sawtimber estimates which were prone to higher adjustments in tree volume.

A relative standard of accuracy has been incorporated into the forest survey. This standard satisfies user demands, minimizes human and instrumental sources of error, and keeps costs within prescribed limits. The two primary types of error are measurement error and sampling error.

Measurement Error

There are three elements of measurement error: (1) bias, which is caused by instruments not properly calibrated; (2) compensating, which is caused by instruments of moderate precision; and (3) accidental, which is caused by human error in measuring and compiling. All of these are held to a minimum by a system that incorporates training, check plots, and editing and checking for consistency. Editing checks in the office screen out logical and data entry errors for all plots. It is not possible to determine measurement error statistically, only hold it to a minimum.

Sampling Error

Sampling error is associated with the natural and expected deviation of the sample from the true population mean. This deviation is susceptible to a mathematical evaluation of the probability of error. Sample errors (in percent) and associated confidence intervals around the sample estimates for timberland area, inventory volumes, and components of change are presented in the following table. The confidence interval refers to the two-out-of-three (67 percent) chance that the true population value obtained from a 100-percent census is within the limits indicated.

Item	Sample estimate and confidence interval		Sampling error
			percent
Forest land (*1,000 acres*)	19,622.4 ±	119.7	0.61
Timberland (*1,000 acres*)	19,536.0 ±	121.1	0.62
All live (*million cubic feet*)			
Inventory	29,510.1 ±	424.9	1.44
Net annual growth	1,387.7 ±	30.5	2.20
Annual removals	1,084.1 ±	34.7	3.20
Annual mortality	344.2 ±	12.1	3.52
Growing stock (*million cubic feet*)			
Inventory	26,049.1 ±	398.6	1.53
Net annual growth	1,247.2 ±	29.1	2.33
Annual removals	985.0 ±	32.1	3.26
Annual mortality	273.7 ±	10.6	3.88
Sawtimber (*million board feet*)			
Inventory	95,095.1 ±	1,997.0	2.10
Net annual growth	4,643.3 ±	130.0	2.80
Annual removals	3,554.3 ±	139.7	3.93
Annual mortality	992.5 ±	47.6	4.80

FIA inventories supported by the full complement of sample plots are designed to achieve reliable statistics for the region. Sampling error increases as the area or volume considered decreases in magnitude. Sampling errors and associated confidence intervals are often unacceptably high for small components of the total resource. Statistical confidence may be computed for any subdivision of the region using the following formula. Sampling errors obtained by this method are only approximations

of reliability because this process assumes constant variance across all subdivisions of totals.

$$SE_s = SE_t \frac{\sqrt{X_t}}{\sqrt{X_s}}$$

Recreational area on the Tombigbee National Forest, Mississippi.
(photo by Sonja N. Oswalt)

where

SE_s = sampling error for subdivision of survey unit or State total

SE_t = sampling error for survey unit or State total

X_s = sum of values for the variable of interest (area or volume) for subdivision of survey unit or State

X_t = total area or volume for survey unit or State

For example, the estimate of sampling error for softwood live-tree volume on Mississippi timberland is computed as:

$$SE_s = 1.44 \frac{\sqrt{29,509.9}}{\sqrt{13,101.7}} = 2.16$$

Thus, the sampling error is 2.16 percent, and the resulting confidence interval (two times out of three) for softwood live-tree volume on Mississippi's national forest timberland is 13,101.7 ± 283.0 million cubic feet. Additional estimates and associated sampling errors may be obtained using the online tool "EVALIDATOR," available at the Web site: http://www.ncrs2.fs.fed.us/4801/fiadb/fim30/wcfim30.asp. Sampling errors in this report may differ slightly from EVALIDATOR errors due to rounding error.

Precautions

Users are cautioned to be aware of the highly variable accuracy and questionable reliability of small subsets of the data, e.g., volume estimates by county. When summarizing statistics from the FIA database, users should familiarize themselves with the procedures to compute sampling error as outlined above.

Table C.1—Total area by survey unit, land class, and census water, Mississippi, 2006

Survey unit	Total area[a]	Forest land				Other land	Census water
		Total forest	Timber-land	Other	Reserved other		
				thousand acres			
Delta	5,585.6	1,745.2	1,734.9	5.9	4.4	3,689.1	151.3
North	8,406.2	5,244.9	5,206.6	10.3	28.0	2,998.4	162.9
Central	5,939.9	4,594.3	4,577.4	10.7	6.2	1,290.0	55.6
South	6,648.5	4,729.7	4,719.3	5.9	4.5	1,367.3	551.6
Southwest	4,415.1	3,308.3	3,297.7	10.5	0.0	1,058.8	48.0
All units	30,995.3	19,622.4	19,536.0	43.3	43.2	10,403.6	969.3

Numbers in rows and columns may not sum to totals due to rounding.
0.0 = a value of >0.0 but <0.05 for the cell.
[a] From the Bureau of the Census, 2005.

Table C.2—Area of timberland by survey unit and ownership class, Mississippi, 2006

Survey unit	All classes	Ownership class			
		National forest	Other public	Forest industry	Nonindustrial private
		thousand acres			
Delta	1,734.9	70.6	199.6	109.4	1,355.3
North	5,206.6	238.0	282.2	343.0	4,343.4
Central	4,577.4	184.2	82.1	568.1	3,743.0
South	4,719.3	602.9	262.3	590.3	3,263.9
Southwest	3,297.7	220.6	110.2	378.7	2,588.3
All units	19,536.0	1,316.1	936.4	1,989.6	15,293.8

Numbers in rows and columns may not sum to totals due to rounding.

Table C.3—Area of timberland by survey unit and forest-type group, Mississippi, 2006

Survey unit	All groups	Forest-type group[a]									
		Longleaf-slash	Loblolly-shortleaf	Pinyon-juniper[b]	Oak-pine	Oak-hickory	Oak-gum-cypress	Elm-ash-cotton-wood	Maple-beech-birch	Exotic hard-wood	Non-stocked
						thousand acres					
Delta	1,734.9	0.0	114.8	0.0	67.8	455.0	564.0	503.1	1.3	0.0	28.9
North	5,206.6	0.0	1,739.1	70.0	555.6	2,102.0	364.7	323.1	7.1	3.1	41.9
Central	4,577.4	12.1	2,150.2	31.0	639.5	1,099.0	497.5	132.2	0.0	4.8	11.1
South	4,719.3	746.7	1,729.9	0.0	636.6	760.2	714.8	62.3	0.0	21.5	47.4
Southwest	3,297.7	1.6	1,353.1	2.8	327.4	940.2	378.2	240.8	0.0	16.2	37.2
All units	19,536.0	760.3	7,087.1	103.8	2,226.9	5,356.5	2,519.2	1,261.5	8.4	45.7	166.5

Numbers in rows and columns may not sum to totals due to rounding.

0.0 = a value of >0.0 but <0.05 for the cell.

[a] Forest-type groups largely based on an algorithm from the tree tally.

[b] Includes eastern redcedar forest type.

Table C.4—Area of timberland by survey unit and stand-size class, Mississippi, 2006

Survey unit	All classes	Stand-size class			
		Saw-timber	Pole-timber	Sapling-seedling	Non-stocked
		thousand acres			
Delta	1,734.9	1,009.3	317.0	379.7	28.9
North	5,206.6	2,318.0	1,382.2	1,464.6	41.9
Central	4,577.4	1,904.3	1,269.1	1,392.5	11.5
South	4,719.3	1,989.1	1,358.6	1,324.2	47.4
Southwest	3,297.7	1,815.5	788.5	656.5	37.2
All units	19,536.0	9,036.2	5,115.4	5,217.4	167.0

Numbers in rows and columns may not sum to totals due to rounding.

Table C.5—Area of timberland by forest-type group, stand origin, and ownership class, Mississippi, 2006

Forest-type group[a] and stand origin	All classes	Ownership class			
		National forest	Other public	Forest industry	Nonindustrial private
		thousand acres			
Softwood types					
Longleaf-slash pine					
Planted	190.2	38.7	18.5	36.5	96.5
Natural	570.1	223	48.7	29.3	269
Total	760.3	261.8	67.2	65.8	365.5
Loblolly-shortleaf pine					
Planted	4,411.6	77.3	69.5	931.9	3,333.0
Natural	2,675.6	389.8	128.6	187.1	1,970.0
Total	7,087.1	467.1	198.0	1,119.0	5,302.9
Pinyon-juniper[b]	103.8	0.0	10.5	0.0	93.3
Total softwoods	7,951.3	728.9	275.8	1,184.8	5,761.8
Hardwood types					
Oak-pine					
Planted	473.6	14.9	16.5	96.0	346.2
Natural	1,753.3	164.3	71.8	88.1	1,429.0
Total	2,226.9	179.2	88.3	184.1	1,775.3
Oak-hickory	5,356.5	270.7	144.9	330.8	4,610.1
Oak-gum-cypress	2,519.2	115.0	299.7	179.3	1,925.3
Elm-ash-cottonwood	1,261.5	11.8	100.9	90.5	1,058.4
Maple-beech-birch	8.4	0.0	0.0	0.0	8.4
Exotic hardwood	45.7	0.0	1.5	0.0	44.2
Total hardwoods	11,418.2	576.6	635.3	784.6	9,421.6
Nonstocked	166.5	10.6	25.4	20.1	110.4
All groups	19,536.0	1,316.1	936.4	1,989.6	15,293.8

Numbers in rows and columns may not sum to totals due to rounding.

0.0 = a value of > 0.0 but < 0.05 for the cell.

[a] Forest-type groups largely based on an algorithm from the tree tally.

[b] Includes eastern redcedar forest type.

Table C.6—Number of live trees on timberland by species group and diameter class, Mississippi, 2006

						Diameter class (inches at breast height)							
Species group	All classes	1.0–2.9	3.0–4.9	5.0–6.9	7.0–8.9	9.0–10.9	11.0–12.9	13.0–14.9	15.0–16.9	17.0–18.9	19.0–20.9	21.0–28.9	29.0 and larger
						thousand trees							
Softwood													
Yellow pine	3,388,427	1,248,470	804,016	596,607	354,326	182,941	96,798	50,265	25,924	12,829	7,721	7,976	554
Other softwoods	200,964	115,308	41,668	18,089	9,809	6,519	3,473	2,025	1,521	977	644	682	249
All softwoods	3,589,391	1,363,778	845,684	614,696	364,135	189,460	100,271	52,290	27,445	13,806	8,365	8,658	803
Hardwood													
Soft hardwoods	5,297,036	3,767,680	833,326	324,064	155,045	88,203	51,626	31,456	19,106	11,271	6,102	8,199	957
Hard hardwoods	4,904,074	3,630,187	660,000	237,996	129,228	77,159	52,456	35,272	25,898	19,047	12,727	19,457	4,647
All hardwoods	10,201,110	7,397,866	1,493,326	562,060	284,274	165,362	104,083	66,727	45,004	30,319	18,829	27,656	5,604
All species	13,790,500	8,761,644	2,339,010	1,176,756	648,408	354,822	204,354	119,018	72,449	44,124	27,194	36,314	6,407

Numbers in rows and columns may not sum to totals due to rounding.

Table C. 7—Number of growing-stock trees on timberland by species group and diameter class, Mississippi, 2006

						Diameter class (inches at breast height)							
Species group	All classes	1.0–2.9	3.0–4.9	5.0–6.9	7.0–8.9	9.0–10.9	11.0–12.9	13.0–14.9	15.0–16.9	17.0–18.9	19.0–20.9	21.0–28.9	29.0 and larger
						thousand trees							
Softwood													
Yellow pine	2,718,411	765,421	687,772	555,396	338,457	175,259	93,604	49,278	25,302	12,331	7,316	7,761	515
Other softwoods	104,427	49,670	24,543	11,552	6,621	4,561	2,764	1,470	1,157	690	609	578	213
All softwoods	2,822,839	815,091	712,315	566,948	345,077	179,820	96,369	50,747	26,459	13,020	7,924	8,339	728
Hardwood													
Soft hardwoods	1,608,727	783,411	361,252	192,979	104,536	64,278	38,852	25,312	16,016	9,441	5,185	6,684	782
Hard hardwoods	1,171,273	526,050	227,816	132,297	85,716	58,953	41,239	29,830	22,609	16,637	10,869	16,188	3,068
All hardwoods	2,780,000	1,309,461	589,068	325,276	190,252	123,232	80,091	55,142	38,625	26,078	16,055	22,872	3,850
All species	5,602,839	2,124,552	1,301,383	892,224	535,330	303,051	176,459	105,889	65,084	39,098	23,979	31,210	4,579

Numbers in rows and columns may not sum to totals due to rounding.

Table C.8—Volume of live trees on timberland by species group and diameter class, Mississippi, 2006

Species group	All classes	Diameter class (*inches at breast height*)									
		5.0–6.9	7.0–8.9	9.0–10.9	11.0–12.9	13.0–14.9	15.0–16.9	17.0–18.9	19.0–20.9	21.0–28.9	29.0 and larger
		million cubic feet									
Softwood											
Yellow pine	12,606.6	1,364.7	2,142.3	2,175.9	1,919.5	1,514.9	1,092.3	762.4	597.4	911.7	125.6
Other softwoods	495.1	42.1	52.5	61.9	54.1	44.9	52.7	45.6	43.1	65.1	33.2
All softwoods	13,101.7	1,406.8	2,194.8	2,237.8	1,973.6	1,559.8	1,144.9	808.0	640.5	976.8	158.8
Hardwood											
Soft hardwoods	6,951.8	808.2	902.0	966.5	914.0	819.0	687.2	539.9	375.3	746.8	193.0
Hard hardwoods	9,456.3	588.1	740.1	848.3	928.7	932.8	972.4	937.7	798.0	1,864.6	845.6
All hardwoods	16,408.1	1,396.3	1,642.0	1,814.9	1,842.7	1,751.8	1,659.6	1,477.5	1,173.3	2,611.4	1,038.6
All species	29,509.9	2,803.1	3,836.8	4,052.7	3,816.2	3,311.6	2,804.5	2,285.5	1,813.8	3,588.2	1,197.4

Numbers in rows and columns may not sum to totals due to rounding.

Table C.9—Volume of growing-stock trees on timberland by species group and diameter class, Mississippi, 2006

Species group	All classes	Diameter class (*inches at breast height*)									
		5.0–6.9	7.0–8.9	9.0–10.9	11.0–12.9	13.0–14.9	15.0–16.9	17.0–18.9	19.0–20.9	21.0–28.9	29.0 and larger
		million cubic feet									
Softwood											
Yellow pine	12,218.3	1,291.7	2,066.5	2,101.1	1,871.2	1,492.5	1,072.6	739.4	573.4	893.0	117.1
Other softwoods	403.9	29.3	38.4	46.4	45.0	35.3	42.1	36.9	40.1	59.9	30.4
All softwoods	12,622.2	1,321.0	2,104.9	2,147.5	1,916.3	1,527.8	1,114.6	776.2	613.5	952.9	147.5
Hardwood											
Soft hardwoods	5,593.1	515.7	653.4	747.9	735.8	696.5	603.3	476.3	337.7	655.4	171.1
Hard hardwoods	7,833.7	365.6	533.8	686.4	771.7	816.8	878.1	851.3	710.3	1,628.4	591.4
All hardwoods	13,426.7	881.3	1,187.1	1,434.3	1,507.5	1,513.3	1,481.3	1,327.6	1,048.0	2,283.8	762.5
All species	26,048.9	2,202.3	3,292.0	3,581.8	3,423.8	3,041.1	2,596.0	2,103.8	1,661.6	3,236.7	910.0

Numbers in rows and columns may not sum to totals due to rounding.

Table C.10—Volume of sawtimber on timberland by species group and diameter class, Mississippi, 2006

		Diameter class (*inches at breast height*)							
Species group	All classes	9.0– 10.9	11.0– 12.9	13.0– 14.9	15.0– 16.9	17.0– 18.9	19.0– 20.9	21.0– 28.9	29.0 and larger
		million board feet[a]							
Softwood									
Yellow pine	44,930.4	7,638.3	8,497.1	7,744.4	6,075.4	4,476.1	3,630.5	6,012.5	856.0
Other softwoods	1,691.2	170.0	194.1	169.7	209.4	191.1	218.4	349.6	188.9
All softwoods	46,621.6	7,808.4	8,691.2	7,914.1	6,284.9	4,667.2	3,848.8	6,362.1	1,044.9
Hardwood									
Soft hardwoods	17,456.3	0.0	2,550.7	2,877.7	2,792.2	2,409.8	1,831.2	3,854.0	1,140.6
Hard hardwoods	31,016.5	0.0	2,754.8	3,386.8	4,025.3	4,197.5	3,705.2	9,222.1	3,724.9
All hardwoods	48,472.8	0.0	5,305.6	6,264.5	6,817.5	6,607.2	5,536.3	13,076.1	4,865.5
All species	95,094.4	7,808.4	13,996.8	14,178.6	13,102.3	11,274.4	9,385.2	19,438.3	5,910.4

Numbers in rows and columns may not sum to totals due to rounding.
0.0 = no sample for the cell.
[a] International 1/4-inch rule.

Table C.11—Volume of live trees on timberland by survey unit and species group, Mississippi, 2006

		Softwoods			Hardwoods		
Survey unit	All species	All softwood	Yellow pine	Other softwood	All hardwood	Soft hardwood	Hard hardwood
		million cubic feet					
Delta	2,844.1	259.2	178.7	80.5	2,584.9	1,207.1	1,377.7
North	7,482.7	2,770.4	2,620.6	149.8	4,712.3	1,718.9	2,993.3
Central	6,932.9	3,875.1	3,832.4	42.8	3,057.8	1,237.3	1,820.5
South	6,350.5	3,657.9	3,560.3	97.6	2,692.6	1,505.0	1,187.5
Southwest	5,899.8	2,539.1	2,414.7	124.4	3,360.6	1,283.4	2,077.3
All units	29,509.9	13,101.7	12,606.6	495.1	16,408.1	6,951.8	9,456.3

Numbers in rows and columns may not sum to totals due to rounding.

Table C.12—Volume of growing stock on timberland by survey unit and species group, Mississippi, 2006

| Survey unit | All species | Softwoods | | | Hardwoods | | |
		All softwood	Yellow pine	Other softwood	All hardwood	Soft hardwood	Hard hardwood
				million cubic feet			
Delta	2,418.4	237.8	166.6	71.2	2,180.5	1,009.3	1,171.3
North	6,439.1	2,622.4	2,523.7	98.7	3,816.7	1,353.7	2,463.0
Central	6,327.7	3,756.5	3,722.4	34.2	2,571.2	997.0	1,574.2
South	5,652.3	3,566.5	3,476.1	90.4	2,085.8	1,179.7	906.1
Southwest	5,211.4	2,438.9	2,329.5	109.4	2,772.5	1,053.4	1,719.2
All units	26,048.9	12,622.2	12,218.3	403.9	13,426.7	5,593.1	7,833.7

Numbers in rows and columns may not sum to totals due to rounding.

Table C.13—Volume of sawtimber on timberland by survey unit and species group, Mississippi, 2006

| Survey unit | All species | Softwoods | | | Hardwoods | | |
		All softwood	Yellow pine	Other softwood	All hardwood	Soft hardwood	Hard hardwood
				million board feet [a]			
Delta	10,158.0	934.3	572.7	361.6	9,223.7	4,141.3	5,082.4
North	22,299.3	8,847.8	8,509.8	338.0	13,451.5	4,024.7	9,426.8
Central	22,624.4	14,169.4	14,034.5	134.9	8,455.0	2,546.0	5,909.0
South	19,465.1	13,224.9	12,892.6	332.3	6,240.3	3,080.3	3,160.0
Southwest	20,547.5	9,445.1	8,920.8	524.3	11,102.4	3,664.0	7,438.4
All units	95,094.4	46,621.6	44,930.4	1,691.2	48,472.8	17,456.3	31,016.5

Numbers in rows and columns may not sum to totals due to rounding.
[a] International 1/4-inch rule.

Table C.14—Volume of live and growing-stock trees on timberland by ownership class and species group, Mississippi, 2006

| | | Softwoods | | | Hardwoods | | |
	All species	All softwood	Yellow pine	Other softwood	All hardwood	Soft hardwood	Hard hardwood
Ownership class							
			Live trees (million cubic feet)				
National forest	3,335.5	1,943.0	1,927.7	15.2	1,392.5	512.9	879.6
Other public	1,766.8	638.5	554.7	83.8	1,128.3	476.1	652.2
Forest industry	2,578.0	1,575.3	1,567.5	7.9	1,002.6	483.4	519.3
Nonindustrial private	21,829.6	8,944.9	8,556.7	388.2	12,884.7	5,479.4	7,405.3
All classes	29,509.9	13,101.7	12,606.6	495.1	16,408.1	6,951.8	9,456.3
			Growing-stock trees (million cubic feet)				
National forest	3,119.8	1,915.9	1,904.9	11.1	1,203.9	424.1	779.8
Other public	1,548.3	617.4	541.5	75.9	931.0	371.5	559.5
Forest industry	2,377.6	1,542.8	1,535.0	7.8	834.8	386.1	448.7
Nonindustrial private	19,003.2	8,546.1	8,236.9	309.2	10,457.2	4,411.4	6,045.7
All classes	26,048.9	12,622.2	12,218.3	403.9	13,426.7	5,593.1	7,833.7

Numbers in rows and columns may not sum to totals due to rounding.

Table C.15—Volume of sawtimber on timberland by ownership class, species group, and size class, Mississippi, 2006

| | | Softwoods | | | Hardwoods | | |
	All species	All softwood	Yellow pine	Other softwood	All hardwood	Soft hardwood	Hard hardwood
Ownership class							
			All size classes (million board feet[a])				
National forest	13,838.2	9,454.6	9,409.9	44.7	4,383.6	1,319.8	3,063.8
Other public	6,758.0	2,905.6	2,553.1	352.5	3,852.3	1,276.5	2,575.8
Forest industry	8,322.2	5,274.5	5,243.2	31.3	3,047.7	1,215.0	1,832.7
Nonindustrial private	66,176.0	28,986.9	27,724.1	1,262.8	37,189.2	13,644.9	23,544.3
All classes	95,094.4	46,621.6	44,930.4	1,691.2	48,472.8	17,456.3	31,016.5
			Trees ≥15.0 inches d.b.h. (million board feet[a])				
National forest	10,128.1	6,787.6	6,768.2	19.4	3,340.5	928.2	2,412.4
Other public	5,079.5	1,924.2	1,625.5	298.7	3,155.3	886.8	2,268.5
Forest industry	4,248.5	1,854.1	1,833.8	20.3	2,394.5	863.4	1,531.1
Nonindustrial private	39,654.4	11,642.1	10,823.1	819.0	28,012.4	9,349.4	18,662.9
All classes	59,110.6	22,207.9	21,050.6	1,157.3	36,902.7	12,027.8	24,874.9

Numbers in rows and columns may not sum to totals due to rounding.
[a] International 1/4-inch rule.

Table C.16—Volume of growing stock on timberland by forest-type group, stand origin, and species group, Mississippi, 2006

Forest-type group[a] and stand origin		Softwoods			Hardwoods		
	All species	All softwood	Yellow pine	Other softwood	All hardwood	Soft hardwood	Hard hardwood
				million cubic feet			
Softwood types							
Longleaf-slash pine							
Planted	219.7	214.7	214.3	0.4	5.0	2.0	3.0
Natural	1,030.2	897.2	885.1	12.1	133.0	90.5	42.5
Total	1,249.9	1,111.9	1,099.4	12.5	138.0	92.5	45.5
Loblolly-shortleaf pine							
Planted	5,202.5	4,949.7	4,945.3	4.4	252.8	144.2	108.6
Natural	5,012.9	4,305.5	4,294.4	11.0	707.4	324.1	383.3
Total	10,215.4	9,255.2	9,239.7	15.4	960.2	468.3	491.9
Pinyon-juniper[b]	51.9	37.4	8.7	28.7	14.5	4.5	10.0
Total softwoods	11,517.2	10,404.5	10,347.9	56.7	1,112.7	565.4	547.3
Hardwood types							
Oak-pine							
Planted	170.9	85.8	85.8	0.0	85.1	27.3	57.8
Natural	2,212.8	1,159.0	1,130.5	28.5	1,053.8	413.9	640.0
Total	2,383.7	1,244.8	1,216.3	28.5	1,138.9	441.2	697.7
Oak-hickory	6,371.9	548.0	495.5	52.5	5,823.9	2,057.6	3,766.3
Oak-gum-cypress	4,391.3	397.7	143.7	254.0	3,993.6	1,581.6	2,412.0
Elm-ash-cottonwood	1,366.7	22.9	11.1	11.8	1,343.8	941.7	402.1
Maple-beech-birch	0.3	0.0	0.0	0.0	0.3	0.3	0.0
Exotic hardwood	14.1	1.8	1.3	0.5	12.3	4.3	8.0
Total hardwoods	14,528.0	2,215.1	1,868.0	347.2	12,312.9	5,026.7	7,286.2
Nonstocked	3.7	2.5	2.5	0.0	1.2	1.0	0.2
All groups	26,048.9	12,622.2	12,218.3	403.9	13,426.7	5,593.1	7,833.7

Numbers in rows and columns may not sum to totals due to rounding.

0.0 = a value of >0.0 but <0.05 for the cell.

[a] Forest-type groups largely based on an algorithm from the tree tally.

[b] Includes eastern redcedar forest type.

Table C.17—Average net annual growth of live trees on timberland by survey unit and species group, Mississippi, 1995 to 2005

Survey unit	All species	Softwoods			Hardwoods		
		All softwood	Yellow pine	Other softwood	All hardwood	Soft hardwood	Hard hardwood
				million cubic feet			
Delta	90.9	14.5	11.7	2.8	76.4	30.6	45.8
North	352.5	180.2	172.2	8.0	172.2	75.3	96.9
Central	381.6	269.1	267.1	2.0	112.5	52.8	59.6
South	296.5	213.5	210.4	3.0	83.1	43.6	39.5
Southwest	266.2	159.1	157.0	2.1	107.1	44.4	62.7
All units	1,387.7	836.4	818.5	17.9	551.2	246.8	304.4

Numbers in rows and columns may not sum to totals due to rounding.

Table C.18—Average net annual growth of growing stock on timberland by survey unit and species group, Mississippi, 1995 to 2005

Survey unit	All species	Softwoods			Hardwoods		
		All softwood	Yellow pine	Other softwood	All hardwood	Soft hardwood	Hard hardwood
				million cubic feet			
Delta	78.8	12.8	10.9	1.9	66.0	24.9	41.1
North	309.2	167.3	161.8	5.5	142.0	59.6	82.3
Central	352.6	257.3	255.6	1.7	95.3	42.0	53.3
South	267.5	205.0	202.6	2.4	62.5	32.5	30.1
Southwest	239.1	151.3	149.6	1.7	87.9	37.3	50.5
All units	1,247.2	793.6	780.5	13.1	453.6	196.3	257.4

Numbers in rows and columns may not sum to totals due to rounding.

Table C.19—Average net annual growth of sawtimber on timberland by survey unit and species group, Mississippi, 1995 to 2005

Survey unit	All species	Softwoods			Hardwoods		
		All softwood	Yellow pine	Other softwood	All hardwood	Soft hardwood	Hard hardwood
				million board feet[a]			
Delta	384.8	46.8	38.0	8.7	338.1	131.1	207.0
North	1,128.6	558.0	536.7	21.3	570.6	202.6	368.0
Central	1,334.1	995.5	988.4	7.1	338.6	107.4	231.2
South	871.2	657.9	650.1	7.7	213.3	101.5	111.9
Southwest	924.5	537.8	526.7	11.2	386.7	149.2	237.5
All units	4,643.3	2,796.0	2,740.0	56.0	1,847.4	691.8	1,155.6

Numbers in rows and columns may not sum to totals due to rounding.
[a] International 1/4-inch rule.

Table C.20—Average annual removals of live trees on timberland by survey unit and species group, Mississippi, 1995 to 2005

Survey unit	All species	Softwoods			Hardwoods		
		All softwood	Yellow pine	Other softwood	All hardwood	Soft hardwood	Hard hardwood
				million cubic feet			
Delta	79.6	4.6	3.9	0.7	75.0	36.7	38.3
North	250.4	126.3	125.1	1.3	124.0	38.6	85.5
Central	290.8	190.5	190.3	0.2	100.3	32.5	67.8
South	254.9	193.1	192.7	0.4	61.7	25.3	36.4
Southwest	208.5	117.4	116.6	0.8	91.1	40.7	50.4
All units	1,084.1	632.0	628.7	3.3	452.1	173.8	278.3

Numbers in rows and columns may not sum to totals due to rounding.

Table C.21—Average annual removals of growing stock on timberland by survey unit and species group, Mississippi, 1995 to 2005

Survey unit	All species	Softwoods			Hardwoods		
		All softwood	Yellow pine	Other softwood	All hardwood	Soft hardwood	Hard hardwood
				million cubic feet			
Delta	66.8	4.4	3.8	0.6	62.4	30.2	32.2
North	220.0	122.5	121.5	1.1	97.5	31.0	66.5
Central	269.5	185.5	185.3	0.2	84.1	26.3	57.7
South	237.2	187.8	187.4	0.4	49.4	20.3	29.0
Southwest	191.5	114.0	113.3	0.7	77.5	35.7	41.9
All units	985.0	614.2	611.3	2.9	370.8	143.5	227.3

Numbers in rows and columns may not sum to totals due to rounding.

Table C.22—Average annual removals of sawtimber on timberland by survey unit and species group, Mississippi, 1995 to 2005

| Survey unit | All species | Softwoods | | | Hardwoods | | |
		All softwood	Yellow pine	Other softwood	All hardwood	Soft hardwood	Hard hardwood
				million board feet[a]			
Delta	310.3	13.6	10.6	3.0	296.7	140.3	156.4
North	715.1	416.7	414.9	1.8	298.4	82.6	215.7
Central	974.6	724.0	723.6	0.4	250.6	53.6	197.0
South	759.8	607.8	607.8	0.0	152.1	54.5	97.6
Southwest	794.5	497.1	493.7	3.4	297.4	116.8	180.5
All units	3,554.3	2,259.2	2,250.6	8.5	1,295.1	447.8	847.3

Numbers in rows and columns may not sum to totals due to rounding.
0.0 = a value of > 0.0 but < 0.05 for the cell.
[a] International 1/4-inch rule.

Table C.23—Average net annual growth and average annual removals of live trees, growing stock, and sawtimber on timberland by species group, Mississippi, 1995 to 2005

| Species group | Live trees | | Growing stock | | Sawtimber | |
	Net annual growth	Annual removals	Net annual growth	Annual removals	Net annual growth	Annual removals
	------------- *million cubic feet* -------------				- - *million board feet*[a] - -	
Softwood						
Yellow pine	818.5	628.7	780.5	611.3	2,740.0	2,250.6
Other softwoods	17.9	3.3	13.1	2.9	56.0	8.5
All softwoods	836.4	632.0	793.6	614.2	2,796.0	2,259.2
Hardwood						
Soft hardwoods	246.8	173.8	196.3	143.5	691.8	447.8
Hard hardwoods	304.4	278.3	257.4	227.3	1,155.6	847.3
All hardwoods	551.2	452.1	453.6	370.8	1,847.4	1,295.1
All species	1,387.7	1,084.1	1,247.2	985.0	4,643.3	3,554.3

Numbers in columns may not sum to totals due to rounding.
[a] International 1/4-inch rule.

Table C.24—Average annual mortality of live trees, growing stock, and sawtimber on timberland by species group, Mississippi, 1995 to 2005

Species group	Live trees	Growing stock	Sawtimber
	million cubic feet		*mmbf[a]*
Softwood			
Yellow pine	131.4	125.2	467.7
Other softwoods	3.2	1.9	5.9
All softwoods	134.6	127.1	473.6
Hardwood			
Soft hardwoods	89.0	63.1	204.2
Hard hardwoods	120.6	83.5	314.7
All hardwoods	209.6	146.6	518.9
All species	344.2	273.7	992.5

Numbers in columns may not sum to totals due to rounding.
[a] International 1/4-inch rule.

Table C.25—Average net annual growth and average annual removals of live trees on timberland by ownership class and species group, Mississippi, 1995 to 2005

Ownership class	All species	Softwoods			Hardwoods		
		All softwood	Yellow pine	Other softwood	All hardwood	Soft hardwood	Hard hardwood
		Average net annual growth *(million cubic feet)*					
National forest	71.4	44.4	44.0	0.4	26.9	14.6	12.4
Other public	62.0	30.7	29.3	1.3	31.3	13.7	17.6
Forest industry	184.3	143.3	142.8	0.6	41.0	23.0	18.0
Nonindustrial private	1,070.0	618.0	602.4	15.6	452.0	195.5	256.5
All classes	1,387.7	836.4	818.5	17.9	551.2	246.8	304.4
		Average annual removals *(million cubic feet)*					
National forest	42.2	33.7	33.5	0.1	8.6	2.6	6.0
Other public	34.0	20.5	20.4	0.1	13.4	6.6	6.8
Forest industry	160.1	118.2	118.0	0.3	41.8	22.6	19.2
Nonindustrial private	847.8	459.6	456.8	2.8	388.3	141.9	246.3
All classes	1,084.1	632.0	628.7	3.3	452.1	173.8	278.3

Numbers in rows and columns may not sum to totals due to rounding.

Table C.26—Average net annual growth and average annual removals of growing stock on timberland by ownership class and species group, Mississippi, 1995 to 2005

		Softwoods			Hardwoods		
Ownership class	All species	All softwood	Yellow pine	Other softwood	All hardwood	Soft hardwood	Hard hardwood
			Average net annual growth *(million cubic feet)*				
National forest	66.8	42.9	42.7	0.2	24.0	13.1	10.8
Other public	55.6	28.8	27.5	1.3	26.8	11.2	15.5
Forest industry	170.2	138.2	137.7	0.5	32.1	17.6	14.5
Nonindustrial private	954.6	583.7	572.6	11.1	370.8	154.3	216.5
All classes	1,247.2	793.6	780.5	13.1	453.6	196.3	257.4
			Average annual removals *(million cubic feet)*				
National forest	40.3	33.2	33.1	0.1	7.1	2.2	4.9
Other public	31.4	19.7	19.6	0.1	11.6	5.8	5.9
Forest industry	149.3	115.3	115.1	0.3	34.0	18.8	15.2
Nonindustrial private	764.0	445.9	443.6	2.4	318.1	116.7	201.4
All classes	985.0	614.2	611.3	2.9	370.8	143.5	227.3

Numbers in rows and columns may not sum to totals due to rounding.

Table C.27—Average net annual growth and average annual removals of sawtimber on timberland by ownership class and species group, Mississippi, 1995 to 2005

		Softwoods			Hardwoods		
Ownership class	All species	All softwood	Yellow pine	Other softwood	All hardwood	Soft hardwood	Hard hardwood
			Average net annual growth *(million board feet[a])*				
National forest	323.1	210.2	209.6	0.6	112.9	54.8	58.1
Other public	288.2	151.8	145.9	6.0	136.4	55.1	81.3
Forest industry	586.1	462.0	461.8	0.2	124.0	67.7	56.3
Nonindustrial private	3,446.0	1,972.0	1,922.7	49.2	1,474.0	514.2	959.8
All classes	4,643.3	2,796.0	2,740.0	56.0	1,847.4	691.8	1,155.6
			Average annual removals *(million board feet[a])*				
National forest	192.4	163.7	163.7	0.0	28.7	5.7	23.0
Other public	148.2	93.8	93.2	0.6	54.4	25.3	29.0
Forest industry	518.5	387.3	387.3	0.0	131.2	73.0	58.2
Nonindustrial private	2,695.2	1,614.4	1,606.4	8.0	1,080.8	343.8	737.1
All classes	3,554.3	2,259.2	2,250.6	8.5	1,295.1	447.8	847.3

Numbers in rows and columns may not sum to totals due to rounding.

0.0 = a value of > 0.0 but < 0.05 for the cell.

[a] International 1/4-inch rule.

Table C.28—Average net annual growth of growing stock on timberland by forest-type group, stand origin, and species group, Mississippi, 1995 to 2005

Forest-type group[a] and stand origin	Softwoods				Hardwoods		
	All species	All softwood	Yellow pine	Other softwood	All hardwood	Soft hardwood	Hard hardwood
				million cubic feet			
Softwood types							
Longleaf-slash pine							
Planted	26.6	25.4	25.3	0.0	1.2	0.6	0.7
Natural	19.2	16.5	16.3	0.2	2.7	1.3	1.4
Total	45.8	41.9	41.7	0.2	3.9	1.8	2.0
Loblolly-shortleaf pine							
Planted	358.2	346.1	346.0	0.1	12.1	6.7	5.4
Natural	189.3	166.0	164.6	1.4	23.3	12.4	10.9
Total	547.5	512.1	510.6	1.5	35.4	19.1	16.3
Pinyon-juniper[b]	0.2	0.2	0.1	0.1	0.0	0.0	0.0
Total softwoods	593.4	554.1	552.3	1.8	39.2	20.9	18.3
Hardwood types							
Oak-pine							
Planted	61.5	45.0	45.0	0.0	16.5	8.6	7.9
Natural	149.9	92.3	90.0	2.3	57.6	25.2	32.5
Total	211.4	137.3	135.0	2.3	74.1	33.7	40.3
Oak-hickory	303.7	84.7	82.5	2.2	219.0	85.3	133.8
Oak-gum-cypress	129.4	16.4	9.6	6.8	113.0	49.8	63.2
Elm-ash-cottonwood	7.8	0.1	0.0	0.1	7.7	6.3	1.4
Maple-beech-birch	0.0	0.0	0.0	0.0	0.0	0.0	0.0
Exotic hardwood	0.3	0.0	0.0	0.0	0.3	0.0	0.3
Total hardwoods	652.6	238.4	227.1	11.3	414.1	175.1	239.0
Nonstocked	1.3	1.0	1.0	0.0	0.2	0.2	0.0
All groups	1,247.2	793.6	780.5	13.1	453.6	196.3	257.4

Numbers in rows and columns may not sum to totals due to rounding.

0.0 = a value of >0.0 but <0.05 for the cell.

[a] Forest-type groups largely based on an algorithm from the tree tally at the beginning of the remeasurement period.

[b] Includes eastern redcedar forest type.

Table C.29—Average annual removals of growing stock on timberland by forest-type group, stand origin, and species group, Mississippi, 1995 to 2005

Forest-type group[a] and stand origin	All species	Softwoods			Hardwoods		
		All softwood	Yellow pine	Other softwood	All hardwood	Soft hardwood	Hard hardwood
				million cubic feet			
Softwood types							
Longleaf-slash pine							
Planted	37.8	37.1	37.1	0.0	0.7	0.1	0.6
Natural	22.1	21.0	20.8	0.2	1.1	0.9	0.2
Total	59.9	58.1	57.9	0.2	1.8	1.0	0.8
Loblolly-shortleaf pine							
Planted	185.5	180.0	179.8	0.2	5.5	2.2	3.3
Natural	244.4	219.4	218.9	0.4	25.1	13.3	11.8
Total	429.9	399.4	398.8	0.6	30.6	15.5	15.1
Pinyon-juniper[b]	0.0	0.0	0.0	0.0	0.0	0.0	0.0
Total softwoods	489.8	457.5	456.7	0.8	32.3	16.5	15.8
Hardwood types							
Oak-pine							
Planted	18.4	13.3	13.3	0.0	5.1	2.2	2.9
Natural	152.9	100.9	100.5	0.4	51.9	15.5	36.4
Total	171.3	114.2	113.8	0.4	57.0	17.7	39.3
Oak-hickory	184.4	34.0	33.4	0.6	150.3	49.9	100.5
Oak-gum-cypress	137.6	8.4	7.4	1.0	129.2	57.8	71.4
Elm-ash-cottonwood	1.9	0.0	0.0	0.0	1.9	1.6	0.3
Maple-beech-birch	0.0	0.0	0.0	0.0	0.0	0.0	0.0
Exotic hardwood	0.0	0.0	0.0	0.0	0.0	0.0	0.0
Total hardwoods	495.1	156.6	154.6	2.1	338.5	127.0	211.5
Nonstocked	0.1	0.1	0.1	0.0	0.0	0.0	0.0
All groups	985.0	614.2	611.3	2.9	370.8	143.5	227.3

Numbers in rows and columns may not sum to totals due to rounding.

0.0 equals a value of > 0.0 but < 0.05 for the cell.

[a] Forest-type groups largely based on an algorithm from the tree tally at the beginning of the remeasurement period.

[b] Includes eastern redcedar forest type.

Table C.30—Average annual output of timber products by product, species group, and type of material, Mississippi, 1995 to 2006

Product and species group	Total output	Round-wood products	Plant byproducts
		million cubic feet	
Saw logs			
Softwood	372.9	367.7	5.2
Hardwood	99.0	98.1	0.9
Total	471.9	465.8	6.1
Veneer logs			
Softwood	62.9	62.9	—
Hardwood	6.5	6.5	—
Total	69.5	69.5	—
Pulpwood			
Softwood	318.9	210.5	108.4
Hardwood	190.2	167.2	23.1
Total	509.1	377.6	131.5
Composite panels			
Softwood	30.0	22.9	7.1
Hardwood	8.7	8.5	0.2
Total	38.7	31.4	7.3
Poles and pilings			
Softwood	8.2	8.2	—
Hardwood	—	—	—
Total	8.2	8.2	—
Other industrial[a]			
Softwood	32.6	0.0	32.6
Hardwood	4.9	—	4.9
Total	37.5	0.0	37.5
Total industrial products			
Softwood	825.6	672.2	153.3
Hardwood	309.4	280.4	29.1
Total	1,135.0	952.6	182.4
Fuelwood[b]			
Softwood	3.1	3.1	0.1
Hardwood	27.5	7.3	0.2
Total	30.6	30.4	0.3
All products			
Softwood	828.7	675.3	153.4
Hardwood	336.9	307.7	29.3
Total	1,165.6	983.0	182.7

Numbers in rows and columns may not sum to totals due to rounding.

— = no sample for the cell; 0.0 = a value of > 0.0 but < 0.05 for the cell.

[a] Includes litter, mulch, particleboard, charcoal, and other specialty products.

[b] Excludes approximately 109.5 million cubic feet of wood residues and 80.6 million cubic feet of bark used for industrial fuel.

Table C.31—Disposal of average annual volume of residue at primary wood-using plants by product, species group, and type of residue, Mississippi, 1995 to 2006

Product and species group	All types	Bark	Coarse[a]	Fine[b]
		million cubic feet		
Fiber products				
Softwood	108.4	—	108.4	—
Hardwood	23.1	—	23.1	—
Total	131.5	—	131.5	—
Particleboard				
Softwood	7.1	—	1.3	5.8
Hardwood	0.2	—	0.1	0.1
Total	7.3	—	1.5	5.8
Sawn products				
Softwood	5.2	—	5.2	—
Hardwood	0.9	—	0.9	—
Total	6.1	—	6.1	—
Industrial fuel				
Softwood	147.9	60.3	5.0	82.6
Hardwood	42.2	20.3	0.7	21.2
Total	190.1	80.6	5.7	103.8
Domestic fuel				
Softwood	0.1	—	0.1	—
Hardwood	0.2	—	0.2	—
Total	0.3	—	0.3	—
Miscellaneous				
Softwood	32.6	8.6	0.4	23.5
Hardwood	4.9	1.6	0.1	3.2
Total	37.5	10.1	0.6	26.8
Not used				
Softwood	5.2	0.6	0.8	3.9
Hardwood	1.1	0.2	0.1	0.7
Total	6.3	0.8	0.9	4.6
All products				
Softwood	306.5	69.4	121.3	115.8
Hardwood	72.5	22.1	25.3	25.2
Total	379.0	91.5	146.5	141.0

Numbers in rows and columns may not sum to totals due to rounding.

— = no sample for the cell.

[a] Material such as slabs and edgings.

[b] Material such as sawdust and shavings.

Table C.32—Average annual output of roundwood products by product, species group, and source of material, Mississippi, 1995 to 2006

Product and species group	All sources	Total	Growing-stock trees[a] Sawtimber *million cubic feet*	Poletimber	Other sources[b]
Saw logs					
Softwood	367.7	349.7	308.9	40.7	18.0
Hardwood	98.1	95.8	89.1	6.7	2.3
Total	465.8	445.5	398.1	47.4	20.3
Veneer logs					
Softwood	62.9	60.7	57.0	3.6	2.3
Hardwood	6.5	6.4	6.4	—	0.1
Total	69.5	67.1	63.4	3.6	2.4
Pulpwood					
Softwood	210.5	130.1	36.5	93.5	80.4
Hardwood	167.2	147.1	86.6	60.6	20.0
Total	377.6	277.2	123.1	154.1	100.4
Composite panels					
Softwood	22.9	19.4	7.0	12.5	3.4
Hardwood	8.5	7.8	4.4	3.4	0.7
Total	31.4	27.3	11.4	15.9	4.1
Poles and pilings					
Softwood	8.2	7.9	6.3	1.6	0.4
Hardwood	—	—	—	—	—
Total	8.2	7.9	6.3	1.6	0.4
Other industrial					
Softwood	0.0	0.0	0.0	0.0	0.0
Hardwood	—	—	—	—	—
Total	0.0	0.0	0.0	0.0	0.0
Total industrial products					
Softwood	672.2	567.8	415.8	152.0	104.5
Hardwood	280.4	257.2	186.5	70.7	23.1
Total	952.6	825.0	602.3	222.7	127.6
Fuelwood					
Softwood	3.1	2.3	1.7	0.7	0.7
Hardwood	27.3	20.3	15.2	5.1	7.0
Total	30.4	22.6	16.9	5.8	7.7
All products					
Softwood	675.3	570.1	417.4	152.7	105.2
Hardwood	307.7	277.5	201.7	75.8	30.1
Total	983.0	847.6	619.2	228.5	135.3

Numbers in rows and columns may not sum to totals due to rounding.

— = no sample for the cell; 0.0 = a value of > 0.0 but < 0.05 for the cell.

[a] On timberland.

[b] Includes trees < 5.0 inches in diameter, tree tops and limbs from timberland, or material from other forest land or nonforest land such as fence rows or suburban areas.

Table C.33—Volume of timber removals by removals class, species group, and source, Mississippi, 1995 to 2006

Removals class and species group	All sources	Source	
		Growing stock	Nongrowing stock
		million cubic feet	
Roundwood products			
Softwood	675.3	570.1	105.2
Hardwood	307.7	277.5	30.1
Total	983.0	847.6	135.3
Logging residues			
Softwood	91.7	33.7	58.0
Hardwood	171.5	57.2	114.3
Total	263.2	90.9	172.3
Other removals			
Softwood	13.9	10.4	3.5
Hardwood	91.4	36.1	55.2
Total	105.3	46.5	58.7
Total removals			
Softwood	780.9	614.2	166.7
Hardwood	570.5	370.8	199.7
Total	1,351.4	985.0	366.4

Numbers in rows and columns may not sum to totals due to rounding.

Table C.34—Average annual timber removals from growing stock on timberland by item, softwood, and hardwood, Mississippi, 1995 to 2006

Item	All species	Softwood	Hardwood
		million cubic feet	
Roundwood products			
Saw logs	445.5	349.7	95.8
Veneer logs and bolts	67.1	60.7	6.4
Pulpwood	277.2	130.1	147.1
Composite panels	7.3	19.4	7.8
Poles and pilings	7.9	7.9	—
Other	0.0	0.0	—
Fuelwood	22.6	2.3	20.3
All products	847.6	570.1	277.5
Logging residues	90.9	33.7	57.2
Other removals	46.5	10.4	36.1
Total removals	985.0	614.2	370.8

Numbers in rows and columns may not sum to totals due to rounding.
— = no sample for the cell; 0.0 = a value of >0.0 but <0.05 for the cell.

Oswalt, Sonja N.; Johnson, Tony G.; Coulston, John W.; Oswalt, Christopher M. 2009. Mississippi's forests, 2006. Resour. Bull. SRS–147. Asheville, NC: U.S. Department of Agriculture Forest Service, Southern Research Station.

Forest land covers 19.6 million acres in Mississippi, or about 65 percent of the land area. The majority of forests are classed as timberland. One hundred and thirty-seven tree species were measured on Mississippi forests in the 2006 inventory. Thirty-six percent of Mississippi's forest land is classified as loblolly-shortleaf pine forest, 27 percent is classified as upland oak-hickory forest, and 19 percent is composed of bottomland hardwoods. Weather-related events were the largest component of average annual disturbance (204,000 acres yearly) on Mississippi forest land since the previous inventory. About 4 percent of live trees on Mississippi's forest land experienced some degree of damage due to Hurricane Katrina.

Keywords: Annual forest inventory, FIA, forest health indicators, forest ownership, Hurricane Katrina, Mississippi, timber volume.

The Forest Service, U.S. Department of Agriculture (USDA), is dedicated to the principle of multiple use management of the Nation's forest resources for sustained yields of wood, water, forage, wildlife, and recreation. Through forestry research, cooperation with the States and private forest owners, and management of the National Forests and National Grasslands, it strives—as directed by Congress—to provide increasingly greater service to a growing Nation.

April 2009

Southern Research Station
200 W.T. Weaver Blvd.
Asheville, NC 28804

Mississippi: The Magnolia State

Capital City: Jackson

Location: 32.32050 N, 090.20759 W

Origin of State's Name: Possibly based on Chippewa Indian words "mici zibi," loosely meaning great river.

Nickname: Magnolia State

Population: 2,730,501; 31st—7-97

Geology:
 Land Area: 47,234 sq.mi.; 32nd
 Highest Point: Woodall Mtn.; 806 feet
 Inland Water: 938 sq.mi.
 Largest City: Jackson
 Lowest Point: Gulf coast; sea level

Border States: Alabama, Arkansas, Louisiana, Tennessee

Coastline: 53 mi.

Constitution: 20th State

Statehood: December 10, 1817

Bird: Mockingbird—Found in all sections of Mississippi, the cheerful Mockingbird was selected as the official State Bird by the Women's Federated Clubs and by the State Legislature in 1944.

Agriculture: Cotton, poultry, cattle, catfish, soybeans, dairy products, rice.

Industry: Apparel, furniture, lumber and wood products, food processing, electrical machinery, transportation equipment.

Natural Resources: Timber, fertile soils, abundant surface water, petroleum, natural gas.

Flag: The committee to design a State Flag was appointed by legislative action February 7, 1894, and provided that the flag reported by the committee should become the official flag. The committee recommended for the flag "one with width two-thirds of its length; with the union square, in width two-thirds of the width of the flag; the ground of the union to be red and a broad blue saltier thereon, bordered with white and emblazoned with thirteen (13) mullets or five-pointed stars, corresponding with the number of the original States of the Union; the field to be divided into three bars of equal width, the upper one blue, the center one white, and the lower one extending the whole length of the flag, red—the national colors; the staff surmounted with a spear-head and a battle-axe below; the flag to be fringed with gold, and the staff gilded with gold."

Tree: Magnolia—An election was held in November 1900 to select a State Flower. Votes were submitted by 23,278 school children. The magnolia received 12,745 votes; the cotton blossom 4,171; and the cape jasmine 2,484. There were a few votes for other flowers. The magnolia was officially designated as the State Flower by the 1952 Legislature. In 1935, the Director of Forestry started a movement by which to select a State Tree for Mississippi, to be selected by nomination and election by the school children of the State. Four nominations were made—the magnolia, oak, pine and dogwood. The magnolia received by far the largest majority. On April 1, 1938, the Mississippi Legislature officially designated the magnolia as the State Tree.

Song: Go, Mississippi
Words and Music by Houston Davis

Flower: Magnolia—An election was held in November 1900 to select a State Flower. Votes were submitted by 23,278 school children. The magnolia received 12,745 votes; the cotton blossom 4,171; and the cape jasmine 2,484. There were a few votes for other flowers. The magnolia was officially designated as the State Flower by the 1952 Legislature. In 1935, the Director of Forestry started a movement by which to select a State Tree for Mississippi, to be selected by nomination and election by the school children of the State. Four nominations were made—the magnolia, oak, pine and dogwood. The magnolia received by far the largest majority. On April 1, 1938, the Mississippi Legislature officially designated the magnolia as the State Tree.

Seal: The present State Seal has been in use since Mississippi became a State in 1817.

Motto: Virtute et armis - By valor and arms

Information courtesy of www.infoplease.com/states, wiki.answers.com.

www.ingramcontent.com/pod-product-compliance
Lightning Source LLC
Chambersburg PA
CBHW081227280526
45787CB00006B/2553

9 781507 582862